MCGRAW-HILL

Microsoft **97**
Access

Timothy J. O'Leary
Arizona State University

Linda I. O'Leary

Irwin
McGraw-Hill

Boston, Massachusetts   Burr Ridge, Illinois   Dubuque, Iowa
Madison, Wisconsin   New York, New York   San Francisco, California   St. Louis, Missouri

Irwin/McGraw-Hill

A Division of The **McGraw·Hill** *Companies*

Microsoft Access 97

This book is printed on acid-free paper.

domestic   4 5 6 7 8 9 0 BAN BAN 9 0 0 9
international   1 2 3 4 5 6 7 8 9 0 BAN BAN 9 0 0 9 8 7

ISBN 0-07-012594-5

The Sponsoring Editor was Rhonda Sands.
The Developmental Editor was Kristin Hepburn.
The Editorial Assistant was Kyle Thomes.
The Marketing Manager was James Rogers.
The Production Supervisor was Richard DeVitto.
The cover was designed by Lorna Lo.
Project management was by Elaine Brett, Fritz/Brett Associates.
Composition was by Pat Rogondino, Rogondino & Associates.
The typeface was ITC Clearface.
Banta Co. was the printer and binder.

Library of Congress Cataloging Card Number 97-72180

When ordering this title, use ISBN 0-07-115473-6

http://www.mhhe.com

Contents

■ ■ ■ ■ ■ ■ ■ ■ ■ ▪ ▪

DBiv

Database Overview

A database is an organized collection of related data. Before computers, most data was kept on paper. Paper records organized in a filing cabinet by name or department are a database. The information in a telephone book, organized alphabetically, is a database. A school's records of teachers, classes, and students are a database.

With computers, the same type of information can be entered and stored electronically using a database application program. The big difference is that an electronic database can manipulate—sort, analyze, and display—the data quickly and efficiently. What took hours of time to pull from the paper files can be extracted in a matter of seconds using a computerized database.

Relational Database Programs

Most microcomputer database programs are relational. These programs organize data into tables consisting of columns (called fields) and rows (called records). For example, a state's motor vehicle department database may have a table consisting of personal information on each vehicle owner, such as their name and address. Each vehicle owner's personal information forms a record. Each record may consist of the following fields of data: first name, last name, street, city, state, zip code, Social Security number, and license number.

The tables in a relational database are related or linked to one another by a common field. For example, the motor vehicle department may have a second database table containing data for each vehicle owned and a third on outstanding citations. The data in one table can then be linked to the data in another table by using a common field, such as the owner's Social Security number or driver's license number. The ability to link database tables creates a relational database (see example below). Relational databases allow you to create smaller and more manageable database tables, since you can combine and extract data between tables.

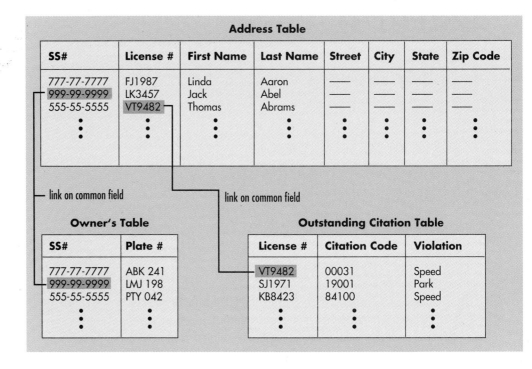

Advantages of Using a Database Program

One of the main advantages of using a computerized database program is the ability to quickly locate specific records. Once you enter data into the database table, you can quickly search the table to locate a specific record based on the data in a field. In a manual system, you can usually locate a record by knowing one key piece of information. For example, if the records are stored in a file cabinet alphabetically by last name, to quickly find a record you must know the last name. In a computerized database, even if the records are sorted or organized by last name, you can still quickly locate a record using information in another field.

A computerized database also makes it easy to add and delete records from the table. Once you locate a record, you can edit the contents of the fields to update the record or delete the record entirely from the table. You can also add new records to a table. When you enter a new record, it is automatically placed in the correct organizational location within the table.

Another advantage of using a computerized database system is its ability to arrange or sort the records in the table according to different fields of data. You can organize records by name, department, pay, class, or any other category you need at a particular time. This ability to produce multiple table arrangements helps provide more meaningful information. The same records can provide information to different departments for different purposes.

A fourth advantage is the ability to analyze the data in a table and perform calculations on different fields of data. Instead of pulling each record from a filing cabinet, recording the piece of data you want to use, and then performing the calculation on the recorded data, you can simply have the database program perform the calculation on all the values in the specified field. Additionally, you can ask questions or query the table to find only certain records that meet specific conditions to be used in the analysis. Information that was once costly and time-consuming to get is now quickly and readily available.

Another advantage of database programs is the ability to quickly produce reports ranging from simple listings to complex, professional-looking reports. You can create a simple report by asking for a listing of specified fields of data and restricting the listing to records meeting designated conditions. You can create a more complex professional report using the same restrictions or conditions as the simple report, but you can display the data in different layout styles, or with titles, headings, subtotals, or totals.

In manual systems, there are often several file cabinets in different departments containing some of the same data. With a computerized database system, more than one department can access the same data. Common updating of the data can be done by any department. The elimination of duplicate information saves both space and time.

Database Terminology

Database: An organized collection of related data that is commonly stored as a table in a file.

Delete: To remove a record from the database file.

Edit: To change or update the data in a field.

Field: The smallest item of information about a record, such as last name.

Query: To ask questions of the database, which then displays only those records meeting specified conditions.

Record: A collection of related fields, such as Social Security number, first name, and last name.

Report: A printed and formatted presentation of specified fields of data for specified records in the file.

Search: To locate a specific record in a file.

Sort: To arrange the records in a file in a specified order.

Table: A collection of data that is organized into columns (fields) and rows (records).

Case Study for Labs 1–5

As a recent college graduate, you have accepted your first job as a management trainee with The Sports Company. This company consists of a chain of sporting goods stores located in large metropolitan areas across the United States. The stores are warehouse oriented, discounting the retail price of most items 15 percent. They stock sporting goods products for all the major sports; basketball, football, tennis, aerobics, and so on.

Your training program emphasis is on computer applications related to retail management. You have been assigned to the Southwest regional office as an assistant to the regional manager and have been asked to suggest how to make the current recordkeeping system of maintaining employee information more efficient.

The company has recently purchased Microsoft Office 97, and you will use the Access 97 database program to computerize the employee records.

In Lab 1 you will learn how to design and create the structure for a computerized database and how to enter and edit records in the database. You will also print a simple report of the records you enter in the database file.

In Lab 2 you will continue to build, modify, and use the employee database of records. You will learn how to sort the records in a database file to make it easier to locate records. Additionally, you will create a customized form to make it easier to enter and edit data in the database file.

In Lab 3 you will learn how to query the database to locate specific information. You will also learn how to use and link multiple tables and create calculated fields.

In Lab 4 you will learn how to use Access 97 to create weekly and monthly employee status reports and mailing labels. The reports will display selected fields of data for the records in the database. They will also include a report title, subgroupings of data, group calculations, and descriptive text to clarify the meaning of the data in the report.

Lab 5 demonstrates the sharing of data between Access and Word. You will learn to import an Access table into a Word document and an Excel spreadsheet, and to perform a mail merge using a Word letter document and an Access table as the data source.

Before You Begin

To the Student
The following assumptions have been made:

- Microsoft Access 97 has been properly installed on the hard disk of your computer system.

- The data disk contains the data files needed to complete the series of labs and practice exercises. These files are supplied by your instructor.

- You have completed the Windows 95 labs or you are already familiar with how to use a mouse and with basic Windows 95 terminology and procedures.

To the Instructor
The following assumptions have been made:

- Microsoft Access 97 has been installed using the default program settings. These settings are in effect each time the program is loaded.

- When the table window is maximized, the number of rows and columns that are displayed varies with the computer system display settings established in Windows. These labs assume a standard VGA display setting (640 x 480), which displays 18 rows. The text and figures reflect this setup.
- The Tip of the Day is not displayed at startup.
- The Office Assistant is on.
- The Advanced Wizards have been installed so that the Input Mask Wizard is available.

Office Shortcut Bar

The Microsoft Office Shortcut Bar (shown below) may be displayed automatically on the Windows 95 desktop. Commonly, it appears in the upper right section of the desktop; however, it may appear in other locations, depending upon your setup. Because the Shortcut Bar can be customized, it may display different buttons than shown below.

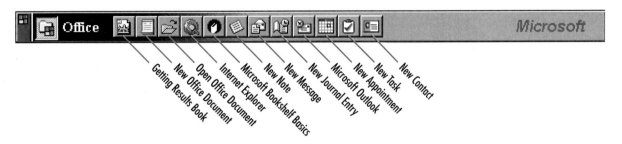

The Office Shortcut Bar makes it easy to open existing documents or to create new documents using one of the Microsoft Office applications. It can also be used to send e-mail, add a task to a to-do list, schedule appointments using Outlook, or add contacts or notes.

Instructional Conventions

This text uses the following instructional conventions:

- Steps that you are to perform are preceded with a bullet (■) and are in blue type. Anything you are to type appears in bold blue type.
- Command sequences you are to issue appear following the word "Choose." Each menu command selection is separated by a /. If the command can be selected by typing a letter of the command, the letter will appear bold and underlined.
- Commands that can be initiated using a button and the mouse appear following the word "Click." The menu equivalent and keyboard shortcut appear in a margin note when the action is first introduced.
- Anything you are to type appears in bold text.

Creating a
Database

1

COMPETENCIES

After completing this lab, you will know how to:

1. Load Access 97.
2. Plan and create a database.
3. Use the Office Assistant.
4. Create a table.
5. Save the table structure.
6. Switch views.
7. Enter and edit data.
8. Adjust column widths.
9. Add records in Data Entry.
10. Preview and print a table.
11. Close and open a database.
12. Exit Access.

CASE STUDY

Currently The Sports Company employee information is maintained on paper forms and stored in file cabinets organized alphabetically by last name. Although the information is well organized, it still takes time to manually leaf through the folders to locate the information you need and to compile reports from this data.

Your current assignment in the management trainee program is to update the employee recordkeeping system to an electronic database management system. A computerized database will not only store and organize the data to make access to the information it contains quick and easy, but allows you to manipulate and present information in a variety of ways.

You will begin by creating an employee database and a table (shown below) of basic employee information.

Employee ID	Date Hired	Last Name	First Name	Street	City	State	Zip Code	Phone Number	Birth Date
0234	4/12/91	Bergstrom	Drew	8943 W. Southern Ave	Mesa	AZ	84101-8475	(602) 555-8201	8/7/61
0434	8/4/91	Long	William	947 S. Forest St.	Tempe	AZ	86301-1288	(602) 555-4494	4/20/70
0728	7/15/91	Toroyan	Lucy	2348 S. Bala Dr.	Tempe	AZ	86301-7985	(602) 555-9870	3/15/61
0839	8/14/91	Artis	Jose	358 Maple Dr.	Scottsd	AZ	85205-8911	(602) 555-0091	12/10/63
1151	10/14/90	Anderson	Susan	4389 S. Hayden Rd.	Mesa	AZ	85205-0346	(602) 555-1950	6/14/65
9999	10/5/98	Student	Name	89 Any Street	Mesa	AZ	85202-9999	(602) 555-5555	8/30/70

Concept Overview

The following concepts will be introduced in this lab:

1. Database Development   The development of a database follows several steps: plan, create, enter data, edit, form design, data analysis, report design, and preview and print.

2. Objects   A database file is made up of many different types of objects, such as tables, forms, and reports.

3. Fields   A field, the smallest unit of information about a record, is identified by a field name.

4. Data Types   The data type defines the type of data the field will contain.

5. Field Properties   Field properties are a set of characteristics that are associated with each field.

6. Primary Key   A primary key is a field that uniquely identifies each record.

7. Views   Access allows you to view objects in your database in several different window formats, called views.

8. Edit and Navigation Modes   The Edit and Navigation modes control how you can move through and make changes to the data in a table.

9. Column Width   Column width refers to the size of each field column in Datasheet view. It controls the amount of data you can see in the column.

Part 1

Loading Access 97

The Sports Company recently purchased the Office 97 application software suite and will use the Access 97 database management program to create several different computerized databases of information. A computerized **database** is an organized collection of information that typically stores the information in tables. A **table** contains data about a specific topic that is organized into vertical columns and horizontal rows. Each row contains a **record**, which is all the information about one person, thing, or place.

You will begin by creating a table using Access 97 to hold the employee data.

■   If necessary, turn on your computer and put your data disk in drive A (or the appropriate drive for your system).

■   Click **Start**.

■   Choose **P**rograms/ Microsoft Access.

Refer to the overview for a complete description of a database.

If a Shortcut to Access 97 button is displayed on your desktop, you can double-click on the button to start the program.

If the Microsoft Office suite is on your system and the Office Shortcut Bar is displayed, you can click the New Office Document button, select Blank Database, and click OK to load Access.

Your screen should be similar to Figure 1-1.

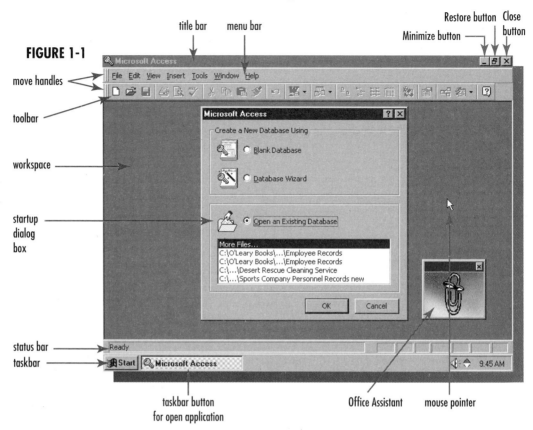

FIGURE 1-1

The Microsoft Access application window with the startup dialog box open should be displayed. The startup dialog box allows you to create a new database or open an existing database. In addition, a small dialog box called the Office Assistant may also be displayed on your screen. The Assistant provides help on any command or window element. You will learn about this feature shortly.

The Access application window includes the same features that are common to the Windows 95 environment: a title bar, menu bar, toolbar, 🗕 Minimize, 🗗 Restore, and 🗙 Close buttons, icons, and mouse compatibility. You can move and size Access windows, select commands, use Help, and switch between files and programs just like in Windows 95. Your knowledge of how to use Windows 95 makes learning about and using Access much easier. The taskbar at the bottom of the screen displays the button for the open application.

The menu bar contains seven menus. The menus and commands that are available at any time vary with the task you are performing.

The toolbar contains buttons that are mouse shortcuts for many menu commands. Many of the buttons are the same as you have seen in toolbars in other Windows 95 applications. Many, however, are specific to Access. Only the first two buttons, ▫ New Database and 🖆 Open Database, and the last one, 🔲 Office Assistant, are currently available for use. All the other buttons are dimmed, indicating they are unavailable. There are 19 toolbars in Access. Most toolbars appear automatically as you perform different tasks and open different windows. The left end of the menu and toolbar displays a **move handle** ║ that when dragged

> Your Office Assistant may display a different character than in Figure 1-1. Do not be concerned if the Assistant is not displayed; you will learn how to display it shortly.

> If necessary, maximize the Access window.

> Pointing to the toolbar buttons displays the button names in a toolbar screen tip.

moves the menu or toolbar to another location. Both menus and toolbars can be docked (as they are now) or floating. When **docked** they are fixed to an edge of the window and display the move handle. When **floating** they appear in a separate window that can be moved by dragging the title bar.

The center area of the window is the **workspace** where different Access windows are displayed as you are using the program. Just below the workspace, the status bar provides information about the task you are working on and the current Access operation. In addition, the status bar displays messages such as button and command descriptions to help you use the program more efficiently.

The mouse pointer appears as an arrow ₖ and operates as in Windows. It also changes shape depending on the task you are performing or its location in the window.

Planning a Database

The Sports Company plans to use Access 97 to maintain several different types of databases. The database you will create will contain information about each Sports Company employee. Other plans for using Access include keeping track of preferred customers and inventory. To keep the different types of information separate, the company plans to create a database for each group. Creating a new database follows several basic steps.

Concept 1: Database Development

The development of a database follows several steps: plan, create, enter data, edit, form design, data analysis, report design, and preview and print.

Plan: The first step in the development of a database is to understand the purpose of the database and to plan what information your database should hold and the output you need from the database.

Create: After planning the database, you create tables to hold data by defining the table structure.

Enter Data: Once a table has been set up, you enter the data to complete each record.

Edit: While entering data, you may make typing and spelling errors that need to be corrected. This is one type of editing. Another is to revise the structure of the tables by adding, deleting, or redefining information in the table.

Form Design: After you create a table, you can create a form for easier data entry. Forms also make editing easier.

Data Analysis: To analyze the data stored in your tables, you ask questions, called queries, of the table data. The results of queries allow you to look at only selected data or to view data in a specific format. For example, you can examine data to determine the largest sales, monthly birthdays, or to make projections.

Report Design: To be able to print your data in a professional and attractive format, you create reports. Reports allow you to customize the appearance of the data.

Preview and Print: The last step is to print a hard copy of the database or report. This step includes previewing the document onscreen as it will appear when printed. Previewing allows you to check the document's overall appearance and to make any final changes needed before printing.

You will find that you will generally follow these steps in order as you create your database. However, you will probably retrace steps as the final database is developed.

DATABASE

Your first step is to plan the design of your database tables: how many tables, what data they will contain, and how they will be related. You need to decide what information each table in the employee database should contain and how it should be structured or laid out.

You can obtain this information by analyzing the current recordkeeping procedures used throughout the company. You need to understand the existing procedures so your database tables will reflect the information that is maintained by different departments. You should be aware of the forms that are the basis for the data entered into the department records, and of the information that is taken from the records to produce periodic reports. You also need to find out what information the department heads would like to be able to obtain from the database that may be too difficult to generate using their current procedures.

After looking over the existing recordkeeping procedures and the reports that are created from the information, you decide to create several separate tables of data in the database file. Creating several smaller tables of related data rather than one large table makes it easier to use the tables and faster to process data. This is because you can join several tables together as needed. The main table will include the employee's basic information, such as employee number, name, and address. Another table will contain job-related information, such as department and job title. A third will contain data on pay rate and hours worked.

Creating a Database

Now that you have decided on the information you want to include in the tables, you are ready to create a new database to hold the table information. From the startup dialog box,

■ Select  **B**lank Database.

■ Click   OK   .

The File New Database dialog box is displayed. The first step is to specify a name for the database file and the location where you want the file saved. By default Access uses the name db1. You want the program to store the database on your data disk using the name Employee Data.

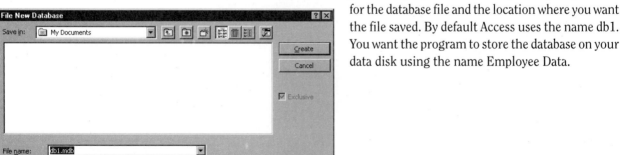

The number in the default file name on your screen may be different.

- If necessary, change the Save In location to the drive containing your data disk.

- Replace the default database file name with Employee Data.

- Click [Create] .

After a few seconds, your screen should be similar to Figure 1-2.

The file name can be entered in either uppercase or lowercase letters, but the name will be stored and displayed the way you type it.

title bar displays database file name and window name

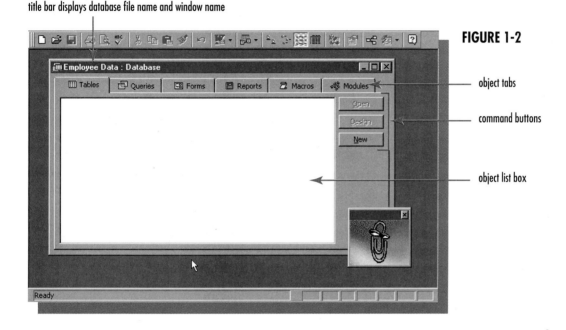

FIGURE 1-2

object tabs

command buttons

object list box

The Database window displays the name of the database, Employee Data, followed by the name of the window in the window title bar. From the Database window you can create and use any database object.

Concept 2: Objects

An **object** is an item, such as a table or report, that is made up of many elements, and that can be created, selected, and manipulated as a unit. The **object tabs** at the top of the Database window are used to select the type of object you want to use. The currently selected object tab is Tables. The table object is the basic unit of a database and must be created first, before any other types of objects are created. The object list box under the object tabs normally displays a list of objects associated with the selected object tab. The Tables object list box is empty because you have not created any tables for this database yet.

Access displays each different type of object in its own window. You can display multiple object windows in the workspace; however, you cannot open more than one database file at a time.

Using the Office Assistant

If the Office Assistant is not displayed, click 🔲 or press F1.

To find out more about tables, you will use the Office Assistant. The **Office Assistant** is used to get Help on features that are specific to the Office application you are using. The Assistant display tips that point out how to use the features or keyboard shortcuts in the program more effectively. A tip is available when a yellow light bulb 💡 appears in the Assistant; click the light bulb to see the tip. It can also automatically display Help suggestions relevant to the specific task you are performing. In addition, you can activate the Assistant at any time to ask for help on any topic. To activate it,

You can also access Help using the Help menu.

■   Click 📎 Office Assistant.

A yellow balloon displays a prompt and a text box in which you can type a question and the Assistant will display a list of topics related to your request. Selecting a topic then will display the Help information on the topic. For Help information about tables,

■   Type **What are tables**

■   Click (● **Search**).

■   Choose Tables: What they are and how they work.

Your screen should be similar to Figure 1-3.

click to move to page 2

FIGURE 1-3

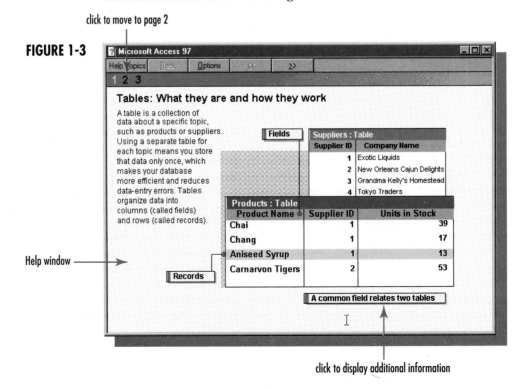

Help window

click to display additional information

Page 1 of three pages of information about tables is displayed. Clicking on the yellow boxes in the window will display additional information about the feature.

- Read the information in the three pages of Help on tables.

- Click ⊠.

Click on the number to move to the next page.

You can leave the Office Assistant open or you can close it and activate it when needed.

- If you want to hide the Assistant, click ⊠ in the Assistant's window.

The illustrations in this text will not display the Assistant open.

Creating a Table

After naming the database, your next step is to create the new table to hold the employee data by defining the structure of the table.

- Click .

The New Table dialog box provides five different ways to create a table. The first three, Datasheet View, Design View, and Table Wizard, are the most commonly used. The Table Wizard option starts the Table Wizard feature, which lets you select from 45 predesigned data-

base tables. The Wizard then creates a table for you based upon your selections. The Datasheet and Design View options open different view windows in which you can create a new custom table from scratch.

You will use the Design View option to create the table.

- Select Design View.

- Click OK.

Access includes 19 different Wizards that can be used to create different Access objects.

You will learn more about views later in the lab.

Your screen should be similar to Figure 1-4.

insertion point

Table Design toolbar ⟶

field definition area ⟶

field properties tabs ⟶

field properties area ⟶

FIGURE 1-4

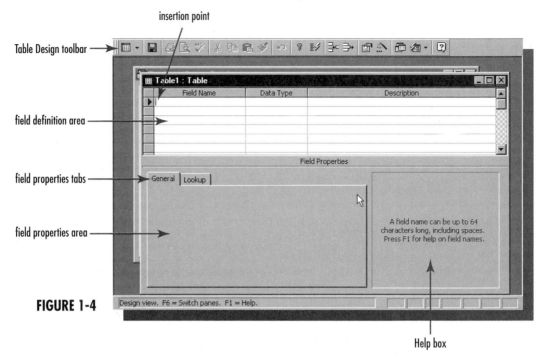

Help box

The Table Design window is opened and displayed over the Database window in the workspace. The Table Design toolbar is also displayed. This toolbar contains the standard buttons as well as buttons (identified below) that are specific to this window.

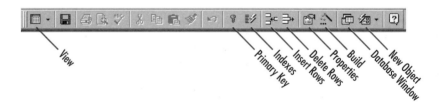

View

Primary Key
Indexes
Insert Rows
Delete Rows
Properties
Build
Database Window
New Object

The upper section of the Table Design window consists of a grid where you define each field to include in the table.

Concept 3: Fields

A **field** is the smallest unit of information about a record. A **field name** is used to identify the data stored in the field. A field name should be descriptive of the contents of the data to be entered in the field. It can be up to 64 characters long and can consist of letters, numbers, spaces, and special characters, except a period, an exclamation point, an accent grave (`` ` ``), and brackets ([]). You also cannot start a field name with a space. Examples of field names are: Last Name, First Name, Address, Phone Number, Department, Hire Date, or other words that describe the data. It is best to use short field names to make the tables easier to manage.

Each row in the grid is where a field is defined by entering the required information in each of the columns. You decide to include the data currently maintained in the personnel folder on each employee in one table using the following 10 fields: Employee ID, Date Hired, Last Name, First Name, Street, City, State, Zip Code, Phone Number, and Birth Date.

In the lower right section of the dialog box, a Help box provides information on the task you are performing in the window. Since the insertion point is positioned in the Field Name text box, the Help box displays a brief description of the rules for entering a valid field name.

The first field of data you will enter in the table is the employee number, which is assigned to each employee when hired. Each new employee is given the next consecutive number, so no two employees can have the same number. It is a maximum of four digits.

■ Type **Employee Number**

Since the data you will enter in this field is a maximum of four characters, you decide to change the field name to Employee ID, so the field name is closer in size to the data that will be entered in the field. To edit the entry,

■ Press [Backspace] (6 times).

■ Type **ID**

■ Press [↵Enter].

The window on your screen should be similar to Figure 1-5.

> The ▶ to the left of the first row indicates the current field.

> The field name can be typed in uppercase or lowercase letters, and will be displayed exactly as entered.

> The [Backspace] key will delete the characters to the left of the insertion point, and the [Delete] key will delete characters to the right.

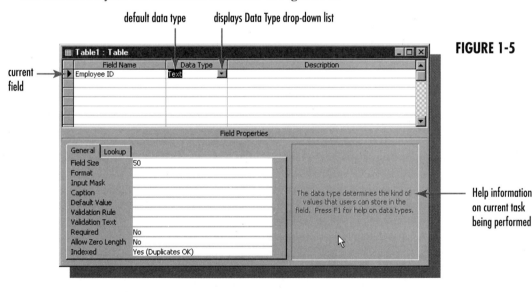

FIGURE 1-5

The insertion point has moved to the Data Type column where the default data type of "Text" is automatically entered.

■ Display the Data Type drop-down list.

Concept 4: Data Types

The **data type** defines the type of data the field will contain. Access uses the data type to ensure that the right kind of data is entered in a field. It is important to choose the right data type for a field before you start entering data in the table. You can change a data type after the field contains data, but if the data types are not compatible, such as a text entry in a field whose data type accepts numbers only, you may lose data. Nine data types are described below.

Data Type	Description
Text	Text entries (words, combinations of words and numbers, numbers that are not used in calculations) up to 255 characters in length (this is the default). Names and phone numbers are examples of Text field entries. Text is the default data type.
Memo	Text that is variable in length and usually too long to be stored in a Text field. A maximum of 65,535 characters can be entered in a Memo field.
Number	Digits only. Number fields are used when you want to perform calculations on the values in the field. Number of Units Ordered is an example of a Number field entry.
Date/Time	Any valid date. Access allows dates from January 1, 100 to December 31, 9999. Access correctly handles leap years and checks all dates for validity.
Currency	Exactly like Number fields, but formatted to display decimal places and a currency symbol.
AutoNumber	A unique, sequential number that is automatically incremented by one whenever a new record is added to a table.
Yes/No	Accepts only Yes/No, True/False, or On/Off entries.
OLE Object	An object, such as a graphic (picture), sound, document, or spreadsheet, that is linked to or embedded in a table.
Hyperlink	Accepts hyperlink entries that are a path to an object, document, Web page, or other destinations.
Lookup Wizard	Displays a list of options you choose from another table in the database. Choosing this data type starts the Lookup Wizard.

A hyperlink is a connection to another document that when clicked on jumps to the referenced location.

Even though a field such as the Employee ID field may contain numeric entries, unless the numbers are used in calculations the field should be assigned the Text data type. This allows other characters, such as the parentheses or hyphens in a telephone number, to be included in the entry. Also, by specifying the type as Text, any leading zeros (for example, in the zip code 07739) will be preserved, whereas leading zeros in a Number type field are dropped (which would make this zip code incorrectly 7739).

To close the Data Type list and accept Text as the data type,

■   Press [Esc].

Also notice in the Field Properties area of the dialog box that the General tab now displays the default field property settings associated with a Text data type.

General	Lookup	
Field Size	50	
Format		
Input Mask		
Caption		
Default Value		
Validation Rule		
Validation Text		
Required	No	
Allow Zero Length	No	
Indexed	Yes (Duplicates OK)	

Concept 5: Field Properties

Field properties are a set of characteristics that are associated with each field. Each data type has a different set of field properties. Setting field properties enhances the way your table works. Some of the more commonly used properties and their functions are described below.

Property	Function
Field Size	Sets the maximum number of characters that can be entered in the field.
Format	Specifies how data displays in a table and prints.
Input Mask	Simplifies data entry by controlling what data is required in a field and how the data is to be displayed.
Caption	Specifies a field label other than the field name.
Default Value	Automatically fills in a certain value for this field in new records as you add to the table. You can override a default value by typing a new value into the field.
Validation Rule	Limits data entered in a field to values that meet certain requirements.
Validation Text	Specifies the message to be displayed when the associated Validation Rule is not satisfied.
Required	Specifies whether or not a value must be entered in a field.
Allow Zero Length	Specifies whether or not an entry containing no characters is valid.
Indexed	Sets a field as an index field (a field that controls the order of records). Speeds up searches on fields that are searched frequently.

You need to set the **field size** for the Employee ID field. By default Access sets a Text field size to 50. Although Access uses only the amount of storage space necessary for the text you actually store in a Text field, setting the field size to the smallest possible size can decrease the processing time required by the program. Additionally, if the field data to be entered is a specific size, setting the field size to that number restricts the entry to the maximum number. Since the Employee ID field will contain a maximum of four characters, you want to change the field size from the default of 50 to 4.

■ Click the Field Size property text box.

■ Replace the default entry with the number 4.

This is the only field property that you want to change. To continue defining the Employee ID field, you will enter a description of the field in the Description text box. Although it is optional, a field description makes the table easier to under-

You can also press F6 to switch between the upper and lower areas of the dialog box.

Clicking on the left edge of the field or property text box when the mouse pointer is a *⇗* will select the entire entry in the box.

stand and update because the description displays in the status bar when you enter data into the table.

> **Text in the Description box scrolls horizontally as needed.**

- ■ Click the Description text box for the Employee ID field.

- ■ Type **A unique 4-digit number assigned to each employee as hired**

Next you want to make this field a primary key field.

Concept 6: Primary Key

A **primary key** is a field that uniquely identifies each record. Most tables have at least one field that is selected as the primary key. The data in the primary key field must be unique for each record. For example, a Social Security number field could be selected as the primary key because the data in that field is unique for each employee. Other examples of a primary key field are parts numbers or catalog numbers.

A primary key prevents duplicate records from being entered in the table and is used to control the order in which records display in the table. This makes it faster for databases to locate records in the table and to process other operations. The primary key is also used to create a link between tables in a database.

Although any field can be the primary key, traditionally the first field or group of fields in the table is the primary key field.

To define the field as a primary key,

> **The menu equivalent is Edit/Primary Key.**

- ■ Click 🔑 Primary Key.

Your screen should be similar to Figure 1-6.

Primary Key button   description

FIGURE 1-6

field properties tabs ———

prohibits duplicate field entries ———

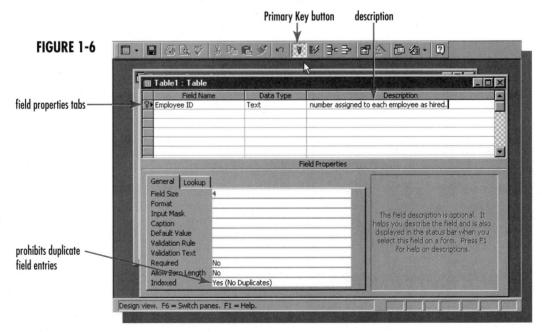

The 🔑 icon appears in the column to the left of the field name, showing that this field is a primary key field. Now that this is the primary key field, the Indexed property setting has changed to Yes (No Duplicates). This setting prohibits duplicate values in a field.

The second field will display the date the employee started working at The Sports Company in the form of month/day/year. To enter the second field name,

- ■ Press ⏎Enter.

- ■ Type **Date Hired**

- ■ Press Tab ⇥ or →.

- ■ Select the Date/Time data type.

The default field properties for the selected data type are displayed. This time you want to change the format of the field so that the date will display as mm/dd/yy, regardless of how it is entered.

- ■ Select the Format property box.

- ■ Open the drop-down list of Format options.

- ■ Choose Short Date.

- ■ In the Description text box of the Date Hired field, enter the description: **Acceptable entry formats are 4/4/99, Apr 4, 1999, or April 4, 1999**

- ■ Press ⏎Enter.

General Date	6/19/94 5:34:23 PM
Long Date	Sunday, June 19, 1994
Medium Date	19-Jun-94
Short Date	6/19/94
Long Time	5:34:23 PM
Medium Time	5:34 PM
Short Time	17:34

The third field is a Text field type that will contain the employee's last name. Because the field name is descriptive of the field contents, a description is not needed.

- ■ Type **Last Name**

- ■ Press ⏎Enter (3 times).

Using Tab ⇥ or → has the same effect as pressing ⏎Enter; it moves the insertion point to the next column to the right. ⇧Shift + Tab ⇥ or ← moves the insertion point to the left one column.

You can also enter the data type by typing the first character of the data type option. For example, you can enter "d" for Date/Time.

You cannot set the field size in Date/Time fields.

■ In the same manner, enter the information shown below for the next seven fields. If you make a typing mistake, use Backspace and Delete to correct errors.

Field Name	Data Type	Description	Field Size/Format
First Name	Text		50
Street	Text		50
City	Text		50
State	Text	A 2-character abbreviation entered in all capital letters.	2
Zip Code	Text	Use the 9-digit zip code if available.	10
Phone Number	Text	Enter using the format (555) 555-5555.	15
Birth Date	Date/Time	Acceptable entry formats are 4/4/99, Apr 4, 1999, or April 4, 1999.	Short Date

You can copy the description from the Date Hired field to the Birth Date field.

When you have completed the seven additional fields, your field definition grid should be similar to Figure 1-7.

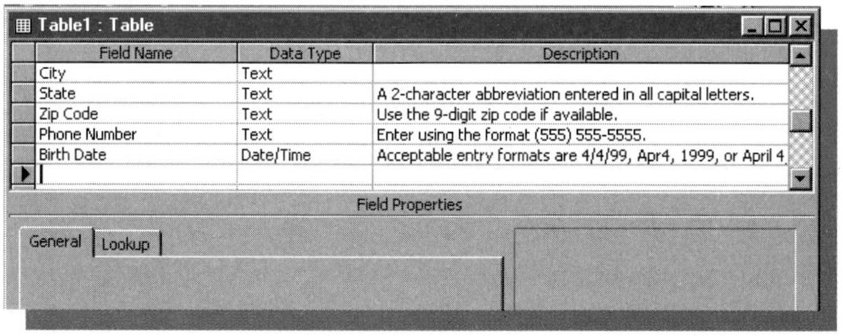

FIGURE 1-7

After looking over the fields, you decide to change the field sizes of the Last Name, First Name, and City fields to 20-character entries. Positioning the insertion point in any column of a field will display the properties for that field.

You may need to scroll the field name grid to see the Last Name field.

■ Move to any column in the Last Name field.

■ Change the field size to 20.

■ In a similar manner, change the field size for the First Name and City fields to 20.

To delete an entire field, move to the field and choose **E**dit/Delete **R**ows.

■ Carefully check your screen to ensure that each field name and field type was entered accurately and make any necessary corrections.

Saving the Table Structure

Once you are satisfied that your field definitions are correct, you can save the
table design by naming it.

The menu equivalent Is **F**ile/**S**ave, and
the keyboard shortcut is Ctrl + S.

■ Click 💾 Save.

In the Save As dialog box, you want to replace the default name, Table 1, with a
more descriptive name. A table name follows the same set of standard naming
conventions or rules that you use when
naming fields. It is acceptable to use the
same name for both a table and the database, although each table in a database
must have a unique name. You will save the table using the table name Employees.

■ Type **Employees**

■ Click OK.

The table structure is saved with the database file. You have created a table named
Employees in the Employee Data database file.

Note: If you are ending your lab session now, follow the directions beginning on
page DB37 to close and open a database and exit Access. When you begin Part 2,
load Access, select Open an Existing Database from the startup dialog box, and
open the file Employee Data from your data disk. Then choose Design from the
Tables tab of the Database window.

Part 2

Switching Views

Now that the table structure is defined and saved, you can enter the employee
data into the new table. You enter and display data in the table in Datasheet view.

Concept 7: Views

Access allows you to view the objects in your database in several different window formats, called
views. The basic views are described in the table below.

View	Use
Design view	Used to create a table, form, query, or report.
Datasheet view	Provides a row-and-column view of the data in tables, forms, and queries.
Form view	Displays the records in a form.
Preview	Displays a form, report, or datasheet as it will appear when printed.

Each view includes it own menu and toolbar designed to work with the object in the window. The
views that are available change depending on the type of object you are working with.

Clicking the ⚊ next to the Table View button displays a drop-down list of available views.

The menu equivalent is **V**iew/Data**s**heet.

The Table View button is a toggle button that switches between the different available views. The graphic in the button changes to indicate the view that will be displayed when selected. The Table View button appears as ☒ for Design view and 🖼 for Datasheet view.

■ Click 🖼 Datasheet View.

Your screen should be similar to Figure 1-8.

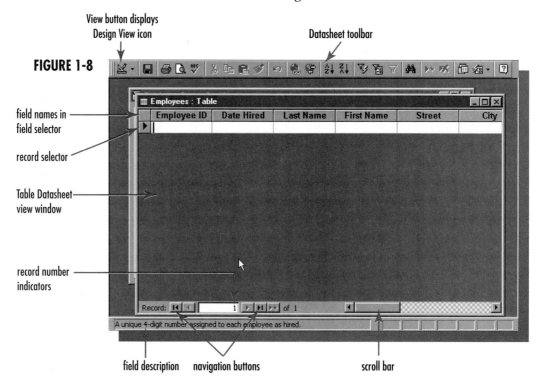

FIGURE 1-8

View button displays Design View icon

Datasheet toolbar

field names in field selector

record selector

Table Datasheet view window

record number indicators

field description   navigation buttons   scroll bar

In Table Datasheet view you can enter and delete records and edit field data in existing records. In addition, this view automatically displays a Table Datasheet toolbar containing the standard buttons as well as buttons (identified below) that are specific to the Table Datasheet view window.

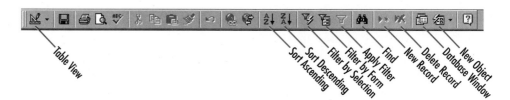

Table View   Sort Ascending   Sort Descending   Filter by Selection   Filter by Form   Apply Filter   Find   New Record   Delete Record   Database Window   New Object

Datasheet view displays the table data in a row-and-column format. Each field is a column of the table. The field names you entered in Design view are displayed as column headings. The column heading area is called the **field selector** for each column. Below the field selector is a blank row where you will enter the data for a record. To the left of the row is the **record selector** symbol ▶, which indicates which record is the **current record**.

The bottom of the window displays a horizontal scroll bar, navigation buttons, and a record number indicator. The **record number indicator** shows the number of the current record as well as the total number of records in the table. Because the table does not yet contain records, the indicator displays "Record: 1 of 1" in anticipation of your first entry. On both sides of the record number are the **navigation buttons**. You use these buttons to move through records with a mouse.

Only the first few field names are visible because there is not enough space in the Employees table window to display all the fields.

■ To see more information in the window, maximize the window.

You will learn about using the navigation buttons in Lab 2.

Now that you can see several more field columns, you notice that the column widths are all the same, even though you set different field sizes in the Table Design window. This is because the Table Datasheet view window has its own default column width setting. You will learn how to change the column width later in this lab.

Entering Data

The insertion point is positioned in the Employee ID field, indicating the program is ready to accept data in this field. The description in the status bar provides the user with information about the data that should be entered in the field. The data you will enter for the first record is as follows:

Field Name	Data
Employee ID	1151
Date Hired	October 14, 1990
Last Name	Anderson
First Name	Susan
Street	4389 S. Hayden Rd.
City	Mesa
State	AZ
Zip Code	85205-0346
Phone Number	(602) 555-1950
Birth Date	June 14, 1965

When you enter data in a record, it should be entered accurately and consistently. The data you enter in a field should be typed exactly as you want it to appear. This is important because any printouts of the data will display the information exactly as entered. It is also important to enter data in a consistent form. For example, if you decide to abbreviate the word "Street" as "St." in the Street field, then it should be abbreviated the same way in every record where it appears. Also be careful not to enter a blank space before or after a field entry. This can cause problems when using the table to locate information.

You will try to enter an Employee ID number that is larger than the field size of 4 that you defined in Table Design view.

■   Type **11510**.

■   Press **←Enter**.

Your screen should be similar to Figure 1-9.

indicates record in process of being entered or edited

indicates a new record

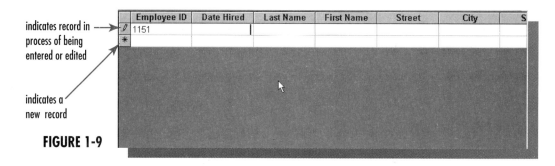

FIGURE 1-9

The program accepted only the first four digits you typed. The field size restriction helps control the accuracy of data by not allowing an entry larger than specified. Also notice that a second row has appeared in the table. The * symbol in the record selector column indicates the end of the table or where a new record can be entered. In addition, the current record symbol has changed to a ▨. This symbol means the record is in the process of being entered or edited and has not yet been saved.

To enter the date hired (it is intentionally incorrect) for this record,

■   Type **10/41/90**

■   Press **←Enter**.

An informational message box is displayed. Access automatically performs some basic checks on the data as it is entered based upon the field type specified in the table design. This is another way Access helps you control data entry to ensure the accuracy of the data. In this case the date entered (10/41/90) could not be correct because there cannot be 41 days in a month. To close the message box,

■   Click **OK**.

Editing Data

Next you need to edit the entry to correct it. How you edit data in Access depends on which mode of operation is active.

Concept 8: Edit and Navigation Modes

The Edit and Navigation modes control how you can move through and make changes to data in a table. **Edit mode** is used to enter or edit data in a field. In Edit mode the insertion point is displayed in the field so you can edit existing data or enter new data. To position the insertion point in the field entry, click at the location where you want it to appear. The keyboard keys shown in the table below can also be used to move the insertion point in Edit mode and to make changes to individual characters in the entry.

Navigation mode is used to move from field to field and to delete an entire field entry. In Navigation mode the entire field entry is selected (highlighted), and the insertion point is not displayed. You move from field to field using the keyboard keys shown in the table below.

Key	Edit Mode
← or →	Moves insertion point left or right one character.
Ctrl + ← or →	Moves insertion point left or right one word.
↓	Move insertion point to current field in next record.
Home or End	Moves insertion point to beginning or end of field in single-line field.
Ctrl + Home or End	Moves insertion point to beginning or end of field in multiple-line field.
Delete	Deletes character to right of insertion point.
Backspace	Deletes character to left of insertion point.
Tab or ⇧Shift + Tab	Ends Edit mode and highlights next or previous field.

Key	Navigation Mode
→ or Tab	Moves highlight to next field.
← or ⇧Shift + Tab	Moves highlight to previous field.
↓	Move highlight to current field in next record.
Home or End	Moves highlight to first or last field in current record.
Delete or Backspace	Deletes highlighted field contents.

To activate Navigation mode, point to the left edge of a field and click when the pointer is a ⊕. To activate Edit mode click on the field when the mouse pointer is an I-beam. To switch between modes using the keyboard, press F2.

Because you are entering data in a new record, Edit mode is automatically active.

If you want to cancel your changes in the current field, press [Esc].

■   Edit the entry to be 10/14/90.

■   Press [←Enter].

The corrected date is accepted, and the insertion point moves to the Last Name field. Because no description was entered for this field, the status bar displays the name of the current view, Datasheet View, instead of a field description.

You can also press [Tab ⇆] to move to the next field. [→] will move to the next field if the insertion point is at the end of the entry or you are in Navigation mode.

The fields will scroll on the screen as you move to the right.

■   Enter the data shown below for the remaining fields, typing the information exactly as it appears.

Field Name	Data
Last Name	**Anderson**
First Name	**Susan**
Street	**4389 S. Hayden Rd.**
City	**Mesa**
State	**AZ**
Zip Code	**85205-0346**
Phone Number	**(602) 555-1950**
Birth Date	**6/14/65**

To complete the record,

■   Press [←Enter].

Your screen should be similar to Figure 1-10.

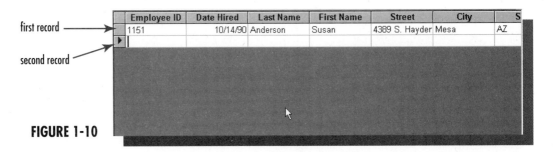

first record

second record

FIGURE 1-10

The data for the first record is complete. The insertion point moves to the first field on the next row and waits for input of the employee number for the next record. As soon as the insertion point moves to another record, the data is saved on the disk and the number of the new record appears in the status bar. The second record was automatically assigned the record number 2.

Record: [I4] [4] [2] [▶] [▶I] [▶*] of 2
A unique 4-digit number assigned to each employee as hired.

Next you will check the first record for accuracy.

You could also press [↑] to move up one record and change to Navigation mode.

■   Point to the left end of the Employee ID field for the first record. When the mouse pointer appears as ⊕, click the mouse button.

The entire field is selected (highlighted), and you have activated Navigation mode. If you type, the entire selection will be replaced with the new text. To select the Street field to check the field contents,

■ Press → (4 times).

■ Click the Street field with the mouse pointer shape as an I-beam.

The insertion point is positioned in the field, and you have activated the Edit mode. Now you can edit the field contents if necessary. To move the insertion point to the end of the address so that you can check the rest of the entry,

■ Press End.

The text scrolled in the field, and the insertion point is positioned at the end of the entry. However, now you cannot see the beginning of the entry. To expand the field box to view the entire entry in the field,

■ Press ⇧ Shift + F2.

> You can also expand a text box in the same way to make it easier to edit.

The entry is fully displayed in a separate zoom window. You can edit in the window just as you would in the field box.

■ If the entry contains an error, correct it.

■ Click OK.

■ Press Tab.

■ Continue to check the first record for accuracy and edit as needed.

■ Enter the following data for the second record.

> You can also use the horizontal scroll bar to scroll the window to check fields that are not visible.

> Notice that the date format changed automatically to the format set in the date property field.

Field Name	Data
Employee ID	0434
Date Hired	June 4, 1991
Last Name	Long
First Name	William
Street	947 S. Forest St.
City	Tempe
State	AZ
Zip Code	86301-1268
Phone Number	(602) 555-4494
Birth Date	April 20, 1970

■ Press ←Enter.

■ Check the second record for accuracy and edit it if necessary.

Your screen should be similar to Figure 1-11.

FIGURE 1-11

second record →

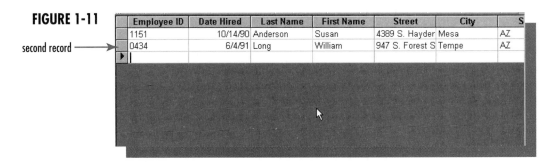

Employee ID	Date Hired	Last Name	First Name	Street	City	S
1151	10/14/90	Anderson	Susan	4389 S. Hayder	Mesa	AZ
0434	6/4/91	Long	William	947 S. Forest S	Tempe	AZ

Adjusting Column Widths

As you have noticed, some of the fields (such as the Street field) do not display the entire entry, while other fields (such as the State field) are much larger than the field's column heading or contents. This is because the default column width in Datasheet view is not the same size as the field sizes you specified in Design view.

Concept 9: Column Width

Column width refers to the size of each field column in Datasheet view. The column width does not affect the amount of data you can enter into a field, but does affect the data that you can see on the screen. The default column width in Datasheet view is set to display 15.6667 characters. You can adjust the column width to change the appearance of the datasheet. It is usually best to adjust the column width so the column is slightly larger than the column heading or longest field contents, whichever is longer. Do not confuse column width with field size. Field size is a property associated with each field; it controls the maximum number of characters that you can enter in the field. If you shorten the field size, you can lose data already entered in the field.

To quickly modify the column width, simply drag the right column border line in either direction to increase or decrease the column width when the mouse pointer shape is ↔. As you drag, a column line appears to show you the new column border. When you release the mouse button, the column width will be set. First you will increase the width of the Street field so the entire address will be visible.

- Point to the right border line of the column heading of the Street field name.

- Drag the border to the right until you think it will be large enough to display the field contents.

- Adjust it again if it is too wide or not wide enough.

You can also adjust the column width to a specific number of characters using Format/Column Width.

Your screen should be similar to Figure 1-12.

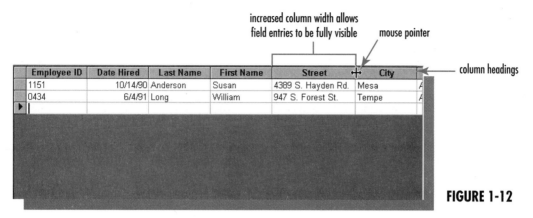

increased column width allows
field entries to be fully visible   mouse pointer

column headings

FIGURE 1-12

Rather than change the widths of all the other columns individually, you can select all columns and change their widths at the same time. To select multiple columns, point to the column heading in the field selector area of the first or last column you want to select. Then, when the mouse pointer changes to ↓, click and without releasing the mouse button drag in either direction across the column headings.

- Point to the Employee ID field name.

- When the mouse pointer is ↓, drag to the right across all column headings.

- Use the horizontal scroll bar to bring the first field column back into view in the window.

Your screen should be similar to Figure 1-13.

selected columns

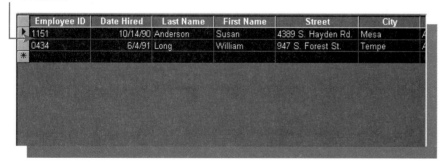

FIGURE 1-13

Multiple columns are highlighted. Now, if you were to drag the column border of any selected column, all the selected columns would change to the same size. However, you want the column widths to be adjusted appropriately to fit the data in each column. To do this you can double-click the column border to activate the Best Fit feature. The **Best Fit** feature automatically adjusts the column widths

To clear a selection, click anywhere in the table.

The fields will scroll horizontally in the window as you drag to select the columns.

The keyboard equivalent for selecting columns is to select a field entry in the first column, press Ctrl + Spacebar, then press ⇧Shift + the appropriate arrow key to select multiple columns.

The menu equivalent is Format/Column Width/Best Fit. The Column Width command is also on the shortcut menu when an entire column is selected.

> Clicking the box to the left of the first field name will select the entire table; however, you cannot use Best Fit when the entire table is selected in this manner.

of all selected columns to accommodate the longest entry or column heading in each of the selected columns.

■ Double-click any selected column border with the mouse pointer as ↔.

Your screen should be similar to Figure 1-14.

column widths adjusted using Best Fit

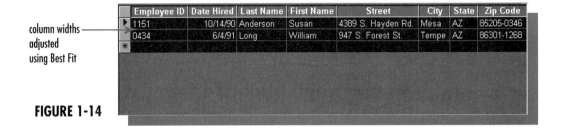

FIGURE 1-14

■ Now that you can see the complete contents of each field, check each of the records again and edit any entries that are incorrect.

■ Add the following record to the table as record 3.

Field	Date
Employee ID	0434
Date Hired	April 12, 1991
Last Name	Bergstrom
First Name	Drew
Street	8943 W. Southern Ave.
City	Mesa
State	AZ
Zip Code	84101-8475
Phone Number	(602) 555-8201
Birth Date	August 7, 1961

■ Press ←Enter.

As soon as you complete the record, an error message dialog box appears indicating that Access has located a duplicate value in a key field. The key field is Employee ID. You realize you were looking at the employee number from the previous record when you entered the employee number for this record. To clear the message and enter the correct number,

- Click [OK].

- Change the Employee ID for record 3 to 0234.

- Press [↓].

The record is accepted with the new employee number. Notice that the address for this record does not fully display in the Street field. It has a longer address than either of the other two records.

- To fully display the Street field data, best fit the field again.

When you add new records in Datasheet view, the records are displayed in the order you enter them. However, they are stored on disk in order by the primary key field. You can change the display on the screen to reflect the correct order by using the [⇧Shift] + [F9] key combination.

- Press [⇧Shift] + [F9].

Your screen should be similar to Figure 1-15.

> Double-click the right border of a field to best fit a single column.

FIGURE 1-15

Employee ID	Date Hired	Last Name	First Name	Street	City	State	Zip Cod
0234	4/12/91	Bergstrom	Drew	8943 W. Southern Ave.	Mesa	AZ	84101-82(
0434	6/4/91	Long	William	947 S. Forest St.	Tempe	AZ	86301-12
1151	10/14/90	Anderson	Susan	4389 S. Hayden Rd.	Mesa	AZ	85205-034

sorted on primary key

The records are now in order by employee number. This is the order determined by the primary key field.

> The table order is also updated when you close and then reopen the table.

Adding Records in Data Entry

Next you want to add several more employee records to the table. Another way to add records is to use the Data Entry command on the Records menu. This command does not display existing records, which prevents accidental changes to the table data.

- Choose **R**ecords/**D**ata Entry.

Your screen should be similar to Figure 1-16.

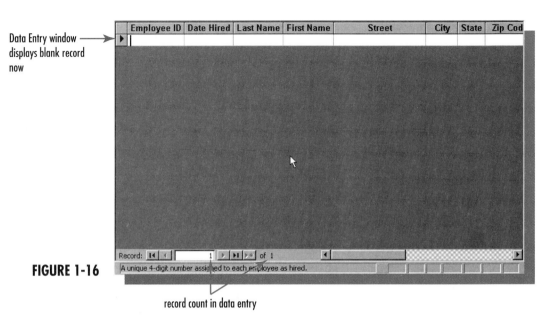

Data Entry window displays blank record now

FIGURE 1-16

record count in data entry

The existing records are hidden and the only row displayed is a blank row where you can enter a new record. The status bar displays "1 of 1." This number reflects the number of new records as they are added in Data Entry rather than all records in the table.

■ Enter the data for the two records shown below.

Field	Record 1	Record 2
Employee ID	0839	0728
Date Hired	August 14, 1991	July 15, 1991
Last Name	Artis	Toroyan
First Name	Jose	Lucy
Street	358 Maple Dr.	2348 S. Bala Dr.
City	Scottsdale	Tempe
State	AZ	AZ
Zip Code	85205-6911	85301-7985
Phone Number	(602) 555-0091	(602) 555-9870
Birth Date	December 10, 1963	March 15, 1961

■ Enter a final record using your first and last name. Enter 9999 as your employee number and the current date as your date hired. The information you enter in all other fields can be fictitious.

- Best fit the City column and any other columns that do not fully display the field contents.

- Check each of the records and correct any entry errors.

Now that you have entered the new records, you can redisplay all the records in the table. To do this,

- Choose **R**ecords/**R**emove Filter/Sort.

Your screen should be similar to Figure 1-17.

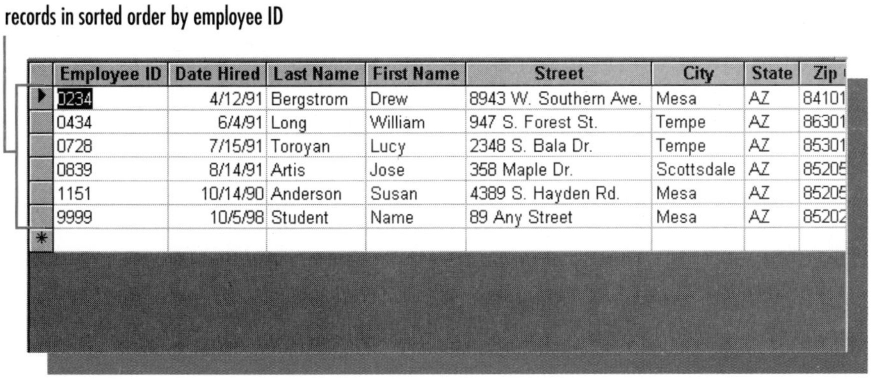

records in sorted order by employee ID

Employee ID	Date Hired	Last Name	First Name	Street	City	State	Zip
0234	4/12/91	Bergstrom	Drew	8943 W. Southern Ave.	Mesa	AZ	84101
0434	6/4/91	Long	William	947 S. Forest St.	Tempe	AZ	86301
0728	7/15/91	Toroyan	Lucy	2348 S. Bala Dr.	Tempe	AZ	85301
0839	8/14/91	Artis	Jose	358 Maple Dr.	Scottsdale	AZ	85205
1151	10/14/90	Anderson	Susan	4389 S. Hayden Rd.	Mesa	AZ	85205
9999	10/5/98	Student	Name	89 Any Street	Mesa	AZ	85202

FIGURE 1-17

The new records are added to the table in order by employee number. If you had added these records in Datasheet view, they would not appear in primary key field order until you updated the table display. This is another advantage of using Data Entry.

Previewing and Printing the Table

If you have printer capability, you can print a copy of the records in this table. Before printing the table, you will preview how it will look when printed using the Print Preview view. Previewing the document displays each page of your document in a reduced size so you can see the layout. Then, if necessary, you can make changes to the layout before printing, to both save time and avoid wasting paper.

To preview the Employee table,

- Click [ ] Print Preview.

The menu equivalent is **F**ile/Print Pre**v**iew.

Your screen should be similar to Figure 1-18.

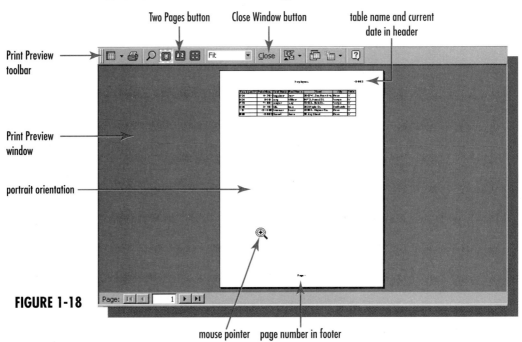

Two Pages button   Close Window button   table name and current
                                           date in header

Print Preview
toolbar

Print Preview
window

portrait orientation

mouse pointer   page number in footer

FIGURE 1-18

The Print Preview window displays a reduced view of how the table will appear when printed. The window also includes its own toolbar.

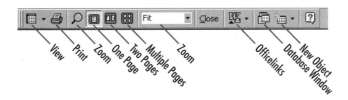

View Print Zoom One Page Two Pages Multiple Pages Zoom Officelinks Database Window New Object

The document will be printed using the default report and page layout settings, which include such items as 1-inch margins, the table name and date displayed in a header, and the page number in a footer. Notice, however, that because the table is too wide to fit across the width of a page, only the first seven fields are displayed on the page. The rest of the table will be printed on a second page. To see both pages,

■ Click ▢▢ Two Pages.

The last three field columns are displayed on the second page. You would like to print the table on a single page. One way to do this is to change the page orientation. **Orientation** refers to the direction text prints on a page. Normal orientation is to print across the width of an 8 1/2-inch page. This is called **portrait** orientation. You can change the orientation to print across the length of the paper. This is called **landscape** orientation. Using landscape orientation lets more information appear on the page because you are printing across the 11-inch length of the paper. To change the orientation to landscape,

- Choose File/Page Setup.

- If necessary, open the Page tab.

- Select Landscape.

- Click OK .

Your screen should be similar to Figure 1-19.

current magnification level

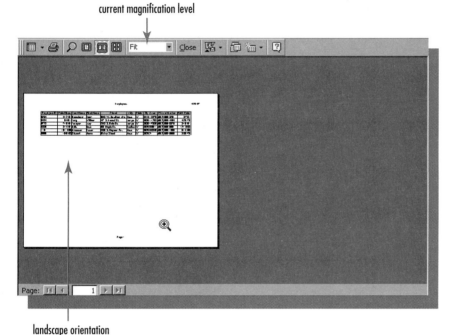

FIGURE 1-19

landscape orientation

Using landscape orientation, the entire table easily fits across the length of the page. To better see the information in the table, you can change the magnification level of the Preview window. The current magnification level is Fit as displayed in the Fit button in the toolbar. This setting adjusts the magnification of the page to best fit in the size of the window. Notice that the mouse pointer is a magnifying glass when it is positioned on the page. This indicates that you can click on the page to switch between the Fit magnification level and the last used level.

- Click on the center of the table.

Use the Fit Zoom button on the Print Preview toolbar to select a magnification percentage or type.

Clicking 🔍 in the toolbar will also toggle between the magnification levels.

Your screen should be similar to Figure 1-20.

current magnification percent
displayed in Zoom button

FIGURE 1-20

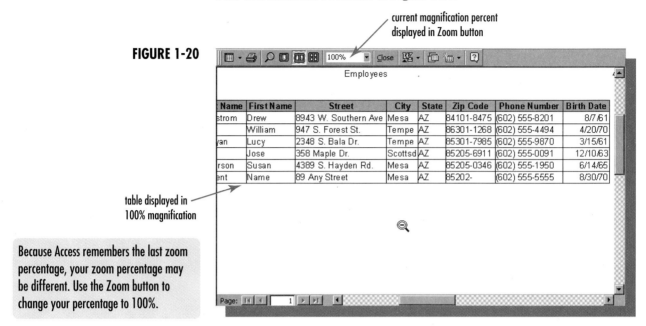

table displayed in
100% magnification

Because Access remembers the last zoom
percentage, your zoom percentage may
be different. Use the Zoom button to
change your percentage to 100%.

The table appears in 100% magnification. This is the size it will appear when printed.

■ Click on the table again to return to the Fit magnification level.

Now you are ready to print the table. The ⊟ Print button on the toolbar will immediately start printing the report using the default print settings. To check the print settings first, you need to use the Print command on the File menu.

■ If necessary, make sure your printer is on and ready to print.

■ Choose File/Print.

The keyboard shortcut for the Print
command is Ctrl + P.

Note: Please consult your instructor for printing procedures that may differ from the directions below.

The Print dialog box on your screen should be similar to Figure 1-21.

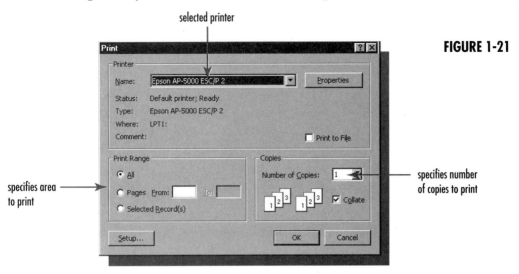

selected printer

FIGURE 1-21

specifies area
to print

specifies number
of copies to print

From this dialog box you need to specify the printer you will be using and the
print settings. The Print Range options are used to specify how much of the
document you want printed. The Copies area of the dialog box is used to specify
the number of copies you want printed. The default settings to print one copy of
the entire document are appropriate.

■ If you need to change the selected printer to another printer, open the Name drop-down list
box and select the appropriate printer (your instructor will tell you which printer to select).

■ Click   OK   .

The printed copy should be the same as displayed in the Print Preview window.
To close the Print Preview window and return to the Datasheet view,

■ Click Close .

The menu equivalent is **V**iew/Data**s**heet
View.

Closing and Opening a Database

To close the table,

■ Click ☒ Close (in the Table window).

The menu equivalent is **F**ile/**C**lose or
Ctrl + W.

Because you changed the column widths of the table in Datasheet view, you are
prompted to save the layout changes you made before the table is closed. If you
do not save the table, your column width settings will be lost.

■ Click   Yes   .

The Database window is displayed again. The name of the table you created appears in the Table object list. Now the Open and Design command buttons can be used to modify the selected table in the list box. To close the database file,

■ Click ⊠ Close (on the menu bar).

Then to open and redisplay the table of employee records,

■ Click 📂 Open Database.

■ If necessary, display the Look-in drop-down list and select the location of your data disk.

The Open dialog box on your screen should be similar to Figure 1-22.

database file name →

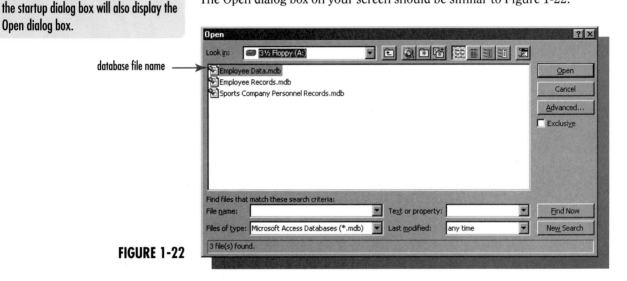

FIGURE 1-22

Now the name of the database file you just created, as well as others you will use in the labs, is displayed in the list box.

■ Select Employee Data.

■ Click [Open].

Then, to open the table of employee records,

■ Click [Open].

The table of employee records is displayed in Datasheet view again, just as it was before you saved and closed the table.

■ Close the table again.

Notice that this time you were not prompted to save the table because you did not make any changes.

Exiting Access

You will continue to build and use the table of employee records in the next lab.
To exit Access and return to the Windows 95 desktop,

Click ⊠ Close (in the Access window title bar).

The menu equivalent is **F**ile/E**x**it, and the keyboard shortcut is Alt + F4.

WARNING!

Do not remove your data disk from the drive until you close the Access application window.

LAB REVIEW

Key Terms

Best Fit   (DB29)
column width   (DB28)
current record   (DB22)
data type   (DB16)
database   (DB7)
docked   (DB9)
Edit mode   (DB25)
field   (DB14)
field name   (DB14)
field property   (DB17)
field selector   (DB22)
field size   (DB17)
floating   (DB9)
landscape   (DB34)
move handle   (DB8)
navigation buttons   (DB23)

Navigation mode   (DB25)
object   (DB11)
object tab   (DB11)
Office Assistant   (DB12)
orientation   (DB34)
portrait   (DB34)
primary key   (DB18)
record   (DB7)
record number indicator   (DB23)
record selector   (DB22)
table   (DB7)
view   (DB21)
workspace   (DB9)

Command Summary

Command	Shortcut	Toolbar	Action
File/**O**pen Database	Ctrl + O		Opens an existing database
File/**N**ew Database	Ctrl + N	□	Creates a new database
File/**C**lose	Ctrl + W	☒	Closes open window
File/**S**ave	Ctrl + S	🖫	Saves table
File/Page Set**u**p/**L**andscape			Changes page orientation to landscape
File/Print Pre**v**iew		🔍	Displays file as it will appear when printed
File/**P**rint	Ctrl + P	🖨	Prints contents of file
File/E**x**it	Alt + F4	☒	Closes Access and returns to Windows 95 desktop
Edit/Delete **R**ows			Deletes selected field in Design view
Edit/Primary **Ke**y		🔑	Defines a field as a primary key field
View/Data**s**heet		▦	Displays table in Datasheet view
F**o**rmat/**C**olumn Width			Changes width of table columns in Datasheet view
F**o**rmat/**C**olumn Width/**B**est Fit			Sizes selected columns to accommodate longest entry or column header
Records/**R**emove Filter/Sort			Displays all records in table
Records/**D**ata Entry			Hides existing records and displays Data Entry window mode

Matching

1. Best Fit _____   **a.** attributes of a field that affect its appearance or behavior

2. database _____   **b.** controls the type of data a field can contain

3. field property _____   **c.** an organized collection of related information

4. primary key _____   **d.** used to define the table structure

5. record _____   **e.** feature used to adjust column width to largest entry

6. field size _____   **f.** collection of related fields

7. field _____   **g.** field used to order records

8. Design view _____   **h.** displays table in row and column format

9. Datasheet view _____   **i.** specific item of information contained in a record

10. data type _____   **j.** controls the maximum number of characters that can be entered in a field

Fill-In Questions

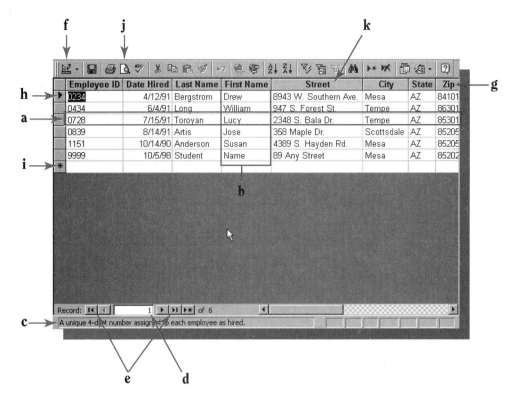

1. Identify the parts of the Access screen by entering the correct term for each item.

a. _____ g. _____

b. _____ h. _____

c. _____ i. _____

d. _____ j. _____

e. _____ k. _____

f. _____

2. Complete the following statements by filling in the blanks with the correct terms.

a. A(n) _____ is a collection of organized information. The information is stored in _____.

b. Relational databases define _____ between tables by having common data in the tables.

c. The first step in developing a database is _____.

d. The _____ defines the type of data that can be entered in a field.

e. A(n) _____ is an item made up of different elements.

f. The set of characteristics associated with a field are the _____.

g. A descriptive label called a(n) _____ is used to identify the data stored in a field.

h. The _____ data type is used to format numbers with dollar signs and decimal places.

i. A(n) _____ is a field that uniquely identifies each record in a table.

j. _____ view allows the user to enter, edit, and delete records in a table.

Discussion Questions

1. Discuss several uses you may have for a relational database. Then explain the steps you would follow to create the first table.

2. Discuss why it is important to plan a database before creating it. How can proper planning save you time later?

3. Discuss the difference between Edit mode and Navigation mode.

4. Design view and Datasheet view are two of the Access views. Discuss when it would be appropriate to use each of these views.

5. Discuss why it is important to choose the correct data type for a field. What may happen to the data if you change the data type?

Hands-On Practice Exercises

Step by Step	**Rating System**	Easy
		☆☆ Moderate
		☆☆☆ Difficult

1. There are many ways to customize the tables you create using Access. In this exercise you will use the Office Assistant to search for information on the ways you can customize Access tables.

a. Open the Access Office Assistant.

b. Request Help information on customizing tables.

c. Based on the Help information you find, list four ways you can customize a table in Design view.

☆☆

2. Debbie started a commercial cleaning business while she was in college. Her business has now grown to a full-service company with four other employees, and she wants to computerize her business records. Debbie wants to start by transferring her client records to Access.

a. Help Debbie create a database named Cleaning Service Records. Design a table using the field information defined below.

Field Data	Type	Field Size	Description
Client #	Text	5	5-digit unique number
Company	Text	50	
Contact	Text	50	First & Last Name of contact person
Address	Text	50	
City	Text	50	
State	Text	2	2-letter abbreviation entered in all capital letters
Zip Code	Text	10	Include the 4-digit extension number if possible
Phone	Text	15	Include the area code in parentheses: (999) 123-4567
Cleaning Day	Text	3	3-letter day code: MON, TUE, WED, THU, FRI, SAT, or SUN
Square Ft	Number		
Rate	Currency		

b. Make the Client # field the primary key field.

c. Change the City field size to 25 and the Contact field size to 40.

d. Save the table as Clients.

e. Enter the following records into the table:

Record 1

95037
St. John & Associates Law Offices
Kelley St. John
13271 N. Central Ave.
Phoenix
AZ
84137-7214
(602) 555-7991
FRI
5000
$150

Record 2

94103
The Sports Company
[your name]
8915 E. Hayden Rd.
Scottsdale
AZ
85254-8211
(602) 555-1294
WED
20000
$500

Record 3

96052
TechnoBabble Electronics
Eddie Fitzpatrick
9860 E. Chandler Blvd.
Chandler
AZ
85601-3144
(602) 555-9876
MON
10000
$250

Record 4

95836
Home Office Supply Co.
Paul Miller
1892 S. Olive Dr.
Phoenix
AZ
89472-8141
(602) 555-1781
TUE
15875
$410

f. Adjust the column widths appropriately.

g. Display the records in primary key order.

h. Preview the table. Change the orientation to landscape. Print, save, and close the table.

3. Michael is the human resources manager for a small working dude ranch resort in Colorado. One of Michael's responsibilities is to maintain employee records. To help him keep track of the employee information, Michael wants to create an Access database.

a. Create a database named Resort Records. Design a table using the field definitions shown below.

Field Name	Data Type	Field Size	Description
Social Security #	Text	11	include hyphens
Last Name	Text	50	
First Name	Text	50	
Middle Initial	Text	1	1 character only
Address	Text	50	Complete street address
City		15	
State		2	
Zip Code		10	complete zip code
Date Hired	Date	Short Date	
Department	Text	50	

b. Make the Social Security # the primary key field.

c. Change the two Name fields sizes to 20, the Address to 30, and Department to 15.

d. Save the table as Staff Records.

e. Enter the following records into the table:

Record 1

015-11-4141
[your last name]
[your first name]
W
34 Maple Dr.
Durango, CO 81301-1131
[current date]
Administration

Record 2

131-31-4199
Johnson
Samantha
T
984 Mountainside Way
Cortez, CO 81205-7100
5/31/95
Housekeeping

Record 3

216-11-2141
Wesley
William
P
9742 S. Gifford Lane
Durango, CO 81301-4141
October 12, 1994
Administration

Record 4

139-99-9891
Feldman
Annie
K
8217 E. Country Rd.
Cortez, CO 81205-7100
2/7/96
Reservations

f. Adjust the column widths appropriately.

g. Display the records in primary key order.

h. Preview and print the table using landscape orientation. Save and close the table.

On Your Own

4. James works at a small office supply store. He needs to create a database to keep track of the store inventory.

Help James create a database named Office Supplies to track item numbers (5-digit unique numbers), item names, quantity on hand, and item cost. The database table, named Inventory, should have a primary key. Enter five sample inventory items into the database. Enter your name in the sixth record item name field. Print the table with the records in primary key order using the appropriate orientation.

5. Michelle owns a small catering business servicing business clients. She has a list of regular clients, and wants to use her computer and Microsoft Access to maintain her client records.

Help Michelle create a database named Catering Business to keep track of her clients. The table, named Customers, should include each customer's identification number, company name, contact person, address, phone number, preferred theme, and favorite dish. Include a primary key field and appropriately size the fields. Enter five records in the table using fictitious data. The last record should include your name. Print the table in primary key order using the appropriate orientation.

6. Create a new database named Lab1PE6 using the Blank Database template. Use the Table Wizard to help you create a table by selecting one of the table samples of your choice from the Personal category. Follow the directions in each step of the Table Wizard and make appropriate selections to create your table. Modify the table design to suit your needs. Add five records to the table. Adjust column widths as needed. Preview, then print your table using the appropriate orientation.

Creating a Database

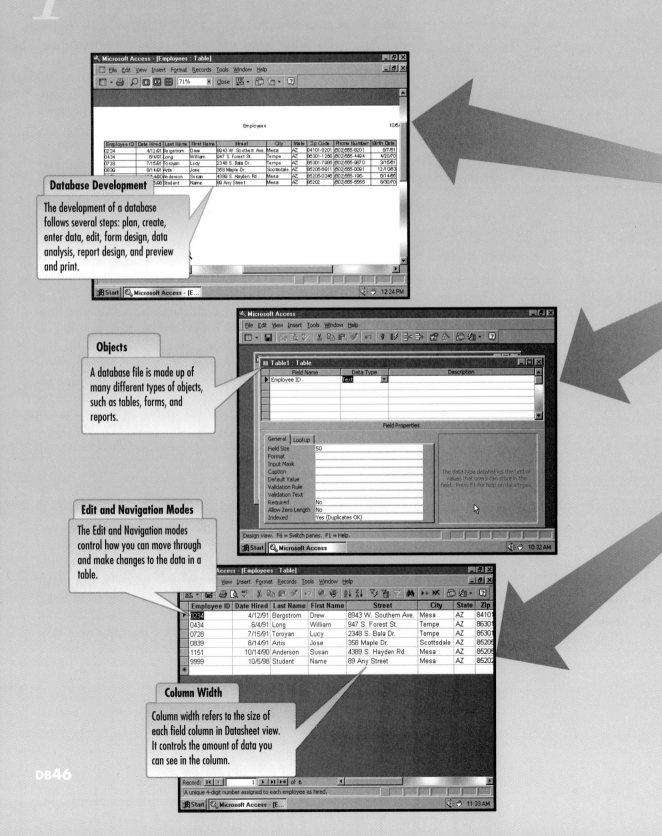

Database Development

The development of a database follows several steps: plan, create, enter data, edit, form design, data analysis, report design, and preview and print.

Objects

A database file is made up of many different types of objects, such as tables, forms, and reports.

Edit and Navigation Modes

The Edit and Navigation modes control how you can move through and make changes to the data in a table.

Column Width

Column width refers to the size of each field column in Datasheet view. It controls the amount of data you can see in the column.

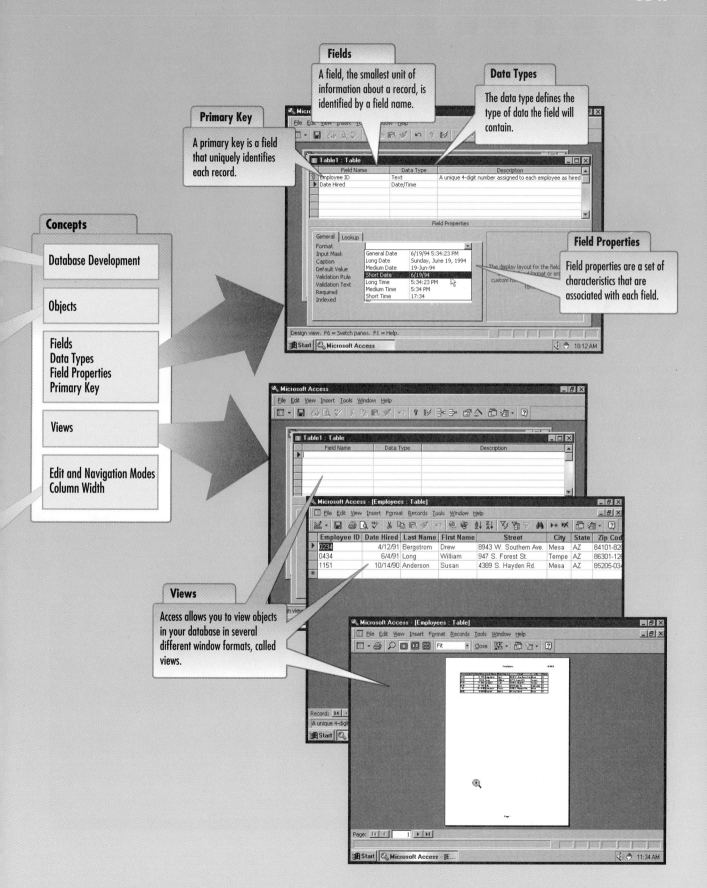

Fields

A field, the smallest unit of information about a record, is identified by a field name.

Data Types

The data type defines the type of data the field will contain.

Primary Key

A primary key is a field that uniquely identifies each record.

Concepts

Database Development

Objects

Fields
Data Types
Field Properties
Primary Key

Views

Edit and Navigation Modes
Column Width

Field Properties

Field properties are a set of characteristics that are associated with each field.

Views

Access allows you to view objects in your database in several different window formats, called views.

Modifying a Table and Creating a Form

CASE STUDY

As you have seen, creating a database takes planning and a lot of time to set up the structure and enter the data. As you have continued to add more employee records to the table, you have noticed several errors. You also realize that you forgot to include a field for the employee's sex. Even with the best of planning and care, errors occur and the information may change. You will see how easy it is to modify the database structure and to customize field properties to provide more control over how and what data is entered in a field.

Even more impressive, as you will see in this lab, is the program's ability to locate information in the database. This is where all the hard work of entering data pays off. With a click of a button you can find data that might otherwise take hours to locate. The end result both saves time and improves the accuracy of the output.

You will also see how you can make the data you are looking at onscreen more pleasing by creating a form (shown here). A form can include colors, text formats, graphic lines and boxes, and layout and design enhancements that greatly improve the onscreen display of information.

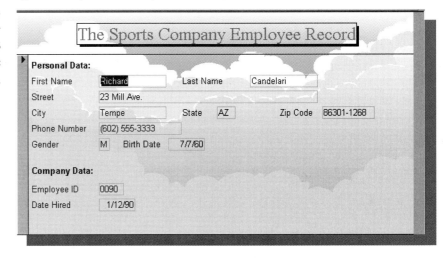

Concept Overview

The following concepts will be introduced in this lab:

1. Format Property — You can use the Format property to create custom formats that change the way numbers, dates, times, and text display and print.

2. Default Value Property — The Default Value property is used to specify a value to be automatically entered in a field when a new record is created.

3. Input Mask Property — An input mask is a pattern that controls the data that can be entered in a field.

4. Find and Replace — The ability to quickly find specific information and automatically replace it with new information is one of the main advantages of a computerized database.

5. Validity Checks — Access automatically performs certain checks, called validity checks, on values entered in a field to make sure that the values are valid for the field type.

6. Sort — You can quickly reorder records in a table by sorting a table to display in a different record order.

7. Forms — Forms are database objects used primarily for data entry and making changes to existing records.

8. Fonts — Fonts consist of three elements: typeface, size, and style that can be applied to characters to improve their appearance.

Part 1

Navigating a Large Table

The database file that contains the additional employee records is on your data disk and is named Employee Records. To open this file,

- Load Access 97. Put your data disk in drive A (or the appropriate drive for your system).
- Select **O**pen an Existing Database.
- Click OK .
- From the Look-in drop-down list box, change the location to the drive containing your data disk.
- Select Employee Records.
- Click Open .

The Database window for the Employee Records file is displayed. To open the table with the additional employee records, Sports Company Employees,

■   Click [Open].

■   Maximize the Datasheet window.

Your screen should be similar to Figure 2-1.

FIGURE 2-1

Employee ID	Date Hired	Last Name	First Name	Street	City	State	Z
0090	1/12/90	Candelari	Richard	23 Mill Ave.	Tempe	AZ	86
0101	2/20/90	Reynolds	Kimberly	8949 S. Summer St.	Tempe	AZ	86
0150	3/5/90	Kennedy	James	5 E. Highland Rd.	Chandler	AZ	83
0151	10/14/90	Anderson	Susan	4389 S. Hayden Rd.	Mesa	AZ	85
0160	3/7/90	Falk	Nancy	470 S. Adams Rd.	Chandler	AZ	83
0230	3/19/90	Dodd	Susan	23 Broadway Rd.	Mesa	AZ	84
0234	4/12/91	Bergstrom	Drew	8943 W. Southern Ave.	Mesa	AZ	84
0367	4/21/91	Steverson	Toni	76 Thomas Rd.	Phoenix	AZ	82
0380	5/12/91	Camalette	Anthony	893 E. McDonald Rd.	Mesa	AZ	84
0434	6/4/91	Long	William	947 S. Forest St.	Tempe	AZ	86
0600	6/10/91	Reynolds	Cara	832 S. William Ave.	Tempe	Az	86
0650	6/15/91	Hanson	Kevin	235 W. Camelback Rd.	Tempe	AZ	85
0728	7/15/91	Toroyan	Lucy	2348 S. Bala Dr.	Tempe	AZ	85
0839	8/14/91	Artis	Jose	358 Maple Dr.	Scottsdale	AZ	85
1142	10/10/91	Spehr	Timothy	90 E. Royal Dr.	Chandler	AZ	83
1151	10/14/90	Anderson	Susan	4389 S. Hayden Rd.	Mesa	AZ	85
1241	1/7/92	Williamson	Anthony	89 College Ave.	Mesa	AZ	84
1260	2/1/92	Little	Jennifer	987 Campus Dr.	Scottsdale	AZ	85

Record: |◄ ◄ [1] ► ►| ►* of 43

navigation buttons   total records

By default, the Datasheet view of the Table window is displayed. As you can see from the record number indicator, there are now 43 records in the table.

In a large table, there are many methods you can use to quickly navigate, or move, through records in Datasheet view. You can always use the mouse to move from one field or record to another. However, if the information is not visible in the window, you must scroll the window first. The table below presents several keyboard methods that make moving around a table faster in Navigation mode.

Keys	Effect
Page Down	Down one page
Page Up	Up one page
Ctrl + Page Up	Left one window
Ctrl + Page Down	Right one window
End	Last field in record
Home	First field in record
Ctrl + End	Last field of last record
Ctrl + Home	First field of first record
Ctrl + ↑	Current field of first record
Ctrl + ↓	Current field of last record

The Navigation buttons in the status bar also provide navigation shortcuts. These buttons also move in Navigation mode and are described below.

Button	Effect
⏮	First record, same field
◀	Previous record, same field
▶	Next record, same field
⏭	Last record, same field
▶*	New (blank) record

You can also type the record number you want to move to in the record indicator box of the status bar.

Currently, records 1 through 18 are displayed in the window. To see the next full window of records,

■ Press Page Down.

Your window may display more records, depending on your monitor settings.

Now records 19 through 36 are displayed in the window. The first record in the window is now the current record.

Due to the number and width of the fields, not all fields can be displayed in the window at the same time. Rather than scrolling the window horizontally to see the additional fields, you can quickly move to the right a window at a time.

■ Press Ctrl + Page Down.

Your screen should be similar to Figure 2-2.

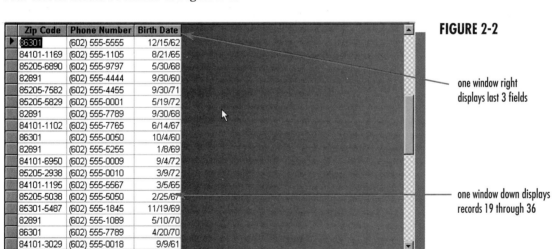

FIGURE 2-2

one window right displays last 3 fields

one window down displays records 19 through 36

The contents of the first field in the window to the right are selected. To quickly move to the same field of the last record and then back to the first field of the first record,

■ Click ⏭.

■ Press Ctrl + Home.

Changing Field Properties

As you viewed the records in the database, you may have noticed that records 11, 22, and 25 have mixed-case entries in the State field. You would like all the state field entries to be in all uppercase letters. Also, rather than having to enter the same state for each record, you want the field to display the state AZ automatically. This will make data entry faster because all the stores are located in Arizona and it is unlikely that the employees will live in another state.

In Lab 1 you set the field properties of several fields. For example, you set the Employee ID field size to 4 so that a larger number could not be entered into the field. In addition, you set the format of the Date Hired field to display a date using the Short Date style. You can also set a field's property to automatically change the entry to uppercase characters. To change the properties of a field, you use Design view.

■   Click [ ] Design View.

■   Make the State field the current field.

The properties associated with the State field are displayed in the General tab. The Format property is used to customize the way an entry is displayed.

Concept 1: Format Property

You can use the Format property to create custom formats that change the way numbers, dates, times, and text display and print. Format properties do not change the way Access stores data, only how the data is displayed.

To change the format of a field, different symbols are entered in the Format text box. Text and Memo Data Types can use any of these four symbols:

Symbol	Description	Example
@	A required text character or space.	@@@-@@-@@@@ would display 123456789 as 123-45-6789. Nine characters or spaces are required.
>	Forces all characters to uppercase.	> would display SMITH whether you entered SMITH, smith, or Smith.
<	Forces all characters to lowercase.	< would display smith whether you entered SMITH, smith, or Smith.
&	An optional text character.	@@-@@& would display 12345 as 12-345 and 12.34 as 12-34. Four out of five characters are required and a fifth is optional.

To enter the symbol to change all entries in the field to uppercase,

- ■ Move to the Format field property text box.

- ■ Type >

Next you want to change the State field property to automatically display the default value of AZ.

Concept 2: Default Value Property

The Default Value property is used to specify a value that is automatically entered in a field when a new record is created. This property is commonly used when most of the entries in a field will be the same for the entire table. That default value is then displayed automatically in the field. When users add a record to the table, they can either accept this value or enter another value. This saves time while entering data.

- ■ Move to the Default Value field property text box.

- ■ Type **AZ**

- ■ Press ⬅Enter.

Your screen should be similar to Figure 2-3.

current field

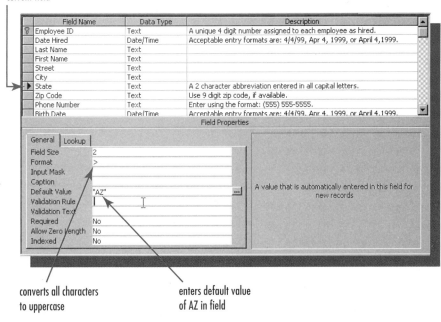

FIGURE 2-3

converts all characters to uppercase

enters default value of AZ in field

The default value is automatically enclosed in quotes to identify the entry as a group of characters called a **character string**.

Creating an Input Mask

While making this change, you decide to change the properties of the Zip Code field to make data entry easier. You want the Zip Code field to display the hyphen and restrict the entry to numbers only. Creating an input mask will set up the field in the desired manner.

Concept 3: Input Mask Property

An **input mask** is a pattern that controls the data that can be entered in a field. It consists of literal characters, which are displayed in the field, and mask characters, which are not. **Literal characters** are characters such as the parentheses surrounding the area code of a telephone number, or a hyphen used to separate the parts of a telephone number. **Mask characters** are symbols that control where the data is entered in the field, the type of data that can be entered, whether the data is required or optional, and the number of characters. They are not displayed in the field and are replaced by the entry as it is typed into the table.

Many of the most common mask characters are described below.

Character	Description
0	A required number entry 0 to 9 (plus (+) and minus (-) signs not allowed)
9	An optional number or space entry (plus and minus signs not allowed)
#	An optional number or space (spaces are displayed as blanks while in Edit mode, but blanks are removed when data is saved; plus and minus signs allowed)
L	A required letter entry (A to Z)
?	An optional letter entry (A to Z)
A	A required letter or digit entry
a	An optional letter or digit entry
&	A required entry of any character or a space
C	An optional entry of any character or a space
.,:;-/	Decimal placeholders and thousands, date, and time separators.
<	Converts all characters to lowercase
>	Converts all characters to uppercase
!	Causes the completed entry in a field to display from right to left, rather than from left to right in the input mask. Characters as you type still fill the input mask from left to right. Use when characters in the input mask are optional. The exclamation point can be entered anywhere in the input mask.
\	Enter before any of the mask characters listed above to have the mask character interpreted as a literal character.

An input mast can have up to three parts, with each part separated by a semicolon. For example, the input mask for a zip code field may be 00000-9999;0;_. The first part, 00000-9999, specifies the input mask itself. The second part, 0, specifies whether the literal display characters are stored in the table when you enter data. If you enter 0 for this section, all literal display characters (for example, the hyphen in a zip code input mask) are stored with the value; if you enter 1 or leave this section blank, only characters you type are stored. The third part specifies the placeholder character that is displayed while entering data to show the space where you should type a character in the input mask. You can specify any character; if this section is left blank, the default displays an underscore. To indicate a blank space, type " " (quote, space, quote).

■ Make the Zip Code field current.

■ Move to the Input Mask field property text box.

Notice that the ■■■ Build button appears to the right of the text box. This button starts the Input Mask Wizard that helps you enter many common input masks as well as create and store your own custom masks.

■ Click ■■■ Build.

■ Click [Yes].

The Input Mask Wizard dialog box on your screen should be similar to Figure 2-4.

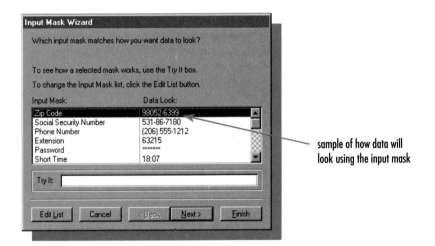

sample of how data will look using the input mask

FIGURE 2-4

> You can also type an input mask directly in the Input Mask text box.

> If the Build ■■■ button is not displayed, the Input Mask Wizard is not installed on your system. Skip to Figure 2.5 and enter the mask shown in the Input Mask text box.

The first Wizard dialog box asks you to select an input mask from the list. The Zip Code input mask is already selected. A sample of how data will appear in the mask is displayed to the right. This looks like how you want the field to appear. To try out this mask,

■ Press [Tab ⇥].

■ Enter your full zip code in the Try It text box (do not include the hyphen).

■ Click [Next >].

> If you do not know your full zip code, enter a ficticious number.

The second Wizard dialog box asks if you want to change the proposed input mask of 00000-9999, and to select the placeholder symbol to display in the mask. The proposed input mask uses zeros to restrict data entry to required numbers for the first five digits of the zip code entry. The last four numbers are optional, therefore 9s are used as the character mask. The hyphen will automatically be entered between the two parts of the zip code. Both the default mask and placeholder of an underscore are acceptable.

■ Click [Next >].

The third Wizard dialog box asks if you want to store the literal (hyphen) as part of the value. This is generally not recommended, because in a large database the extra space consumed by these symbols may become significant. Therefore the proposed response is correct.

- Click Next >.
- Click Finish.
- Press ←Enter.

Your screen should be similar to Figure 2-5.

FIGURE 2-5

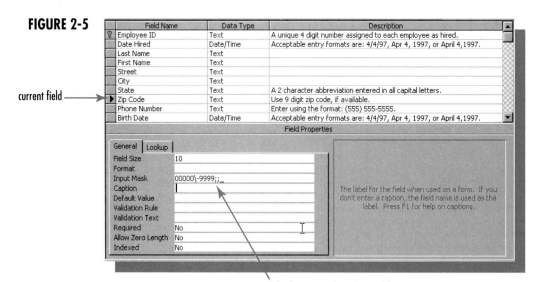

current field →

input mask for five required numbers and four optional

Notice the \ character preceding the hyphen. The program enters the symbol for you to indicate that the hyphen is a literal character to display in the field.

You also decide to make a similar adjustment to the Phone Number field property. Rather than having to type the parentheses and hyphen, you want these characters to automatically display in the field. In addition, you want the field to accept numeric entries only.

> If the Input Mask Wizard is not available, enter the phone number mask directly in the text box.

- Use the Input Mask Wizard to enter the input mask for the Phone Number field.
- Press ←Enter.

When you are done the input mask in this field property should be: \\(999") "000\-0000;;_.

To see how the new field property settings have changed the table,

- Click 🔳 Datasheet View.
- Click Yes.
- Move to the Phone Number field of record 1.

Your screen should be similar to Figure 2-6.

uppercase characters
in State field

input masks applied to Zip Code
and Phone Number fields

FIGURE 2-6

Last Name	First Name	Street	City	State	Zip Code	Phone Number
Candelari	Richard	23 Mill Ave.	Tempe	AZ	86301-	(602) 555-3333
Reynolds	Kimberly	8949 S. Summer St.	Tempe	AZ	86301-	(602) 555-4000
Kennedy	James	5 E. Highland Rd.	Chandler	AZ	83174-2311	(602) 555-5566
Anderson	Susan	4389 S. Hayden Rd.	Mesa	AZ	85205-0346	(602) 555-1950
Falk	Nancy	470 S. Adams Rd.	Chandler	AZ	83174-	(602) 555-7380
Dodd	Susan	23 Broadway Rd.	Mesa	AZ	84101-	(602) 939-3333
Bergstrom	Drew	8943 W. Southern Ave.	Mesa	AZ	84101-8475	(602) 555-8201
Steverson	Toni	76 Thomas Rd.	Phoenix	AZ	82891-	(602) 555-2222
Camalette	Anthony	893 E. McDonald Rd.	Mesa	AZ	84101-	(602) 555-7830
Long	William	947 S. Forest St.	Tempe	AZ	86301-1268	(602) 555-4494
Reynolds	Cara	832 S. William Ave.	Tempe	AZ	86301-	(602) 555-3730
Hanson	Kevin	235 W. Camelback Rd.	Tempe	AZ	85301-	(602) 555-7380

First, notice that the entry in the State field for record 11, Cara Reynolds, which had lowercase characters, has been converted to uppercase characters. This change is a result of the format property setting you entered for the State field. The Zip Code field displays the existing five-digit zip codes followed by the hyphen character as specified by the input mask for that field.

Because the entries in the Phone Number field already include the parentheses and hyphen, it is not possible to see the effect of the input mask on the field. However, when you enter a new record, you will see how this mask helps data entry.

■   Move to a new blank record.

Notice that the new record displays "AZ" as the default value in the State field.

■   To see how the new format and input mask settings affect data input, enter the following new record:

You can click ▶✱ to quickly move to a new blank record.

Field	Data
Employee ID	1388
Date Hired	5/17/92
Last Name	Nelson
First Name	Linda
Address	422 Candy Ln.
City	Phoenix

Because the state for this record is AZ, you can accept the default field value and skip this field. If the state were other than AZ, you could edit the entry.

■   Press ⏎Enter.

Next, in the Zip Code and Phone Number fields, you do not type the hyphens or parentheses, as they are supplied by the input mask. If you enter any characters except numbers in these fields, they will be rejected. Complete the record by entering the data shown below.

Field	Data
Zip Code	828911605
Phone Number	6025557268
Birth Date	9/14/45

You must enter three blank spaces if you do not want to include the area code in the phone number.

To complete this record and return to the first record,

■ Press ←Enter.

■ Click ◄◄.

Finding and Replacing Data

Next you want to update the Zip Code field for the existing records. You have checked with the U.S. Postal Service and found that all zip codes of 82891 have a four-digit extension of 1605. To locate all the records with this zip code, you could look at the Zip Code field for each record to find the match and then edit the field to add the extension. If the table is small, this method would be acceptable. For large tables, however, this method could be quite time consuming and more prone to errors. A more efficient way is to search the table to find specific values in records and then replace the entry with another.

Concept 4: Find and Replace

The Find command will locate all specified values in a field, and the Replace command will both find a value and automatically replace it with another. For example, in a table containing supplier and item prices, you may need to increase the price of all items supplied by one manufacturer. To quickly locate these items, you would use the Find command to locate all records with the name of the manufacturer and then update the price appropriately. Alternatively, you could use the Replace command if you knew that all items priced at $9.95 were increasing to $11.89. This command would locate all values matching the original price and replace them with the new price. Finding and replacing data is fast and accurate, but you need to be careful when replacing not to replace unintended matches.

The Replace command will search the current field to find the specified data and replace it with other data.

■ Move to the Zip Code field of record 1.

■ Choose Edit/Replace.

The keyboard shortcut is Ctrl+H.

The Replace in Field dialog box shows the name of the field it will search (the current field) in the title bar. In the Find What text box you enter the text you want to locate, and in the Replace With text box you enter the replacement text exactly as you want it to appear in your document. You do not include input

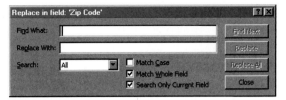

mask literal characters such as hyphens that are entered by the input mask in the replacement text. In the search drop-down list box, you can select All to search all records, or Down or Up to search down or up from the insertion point in the selected field. The other search options you can use to modify how the search is conducted are discussed below.

Option	Effect on Text	Example
Match Case	Finds only those text entries that have the same use of uppercase and lowercase text as the entry in the Find What text box. This option is off by default.	Enter "Southwest" in the Find What text box, turn on Match Case. You would not Locate "southwest."
Match Whole Field	Finds only whole words, not the same text inside longer words. This option is on by default.	Enter "cat" in the Find What text box, turn on Match Whole Field. You would not locate "catastrophe" or "indicate."
Search Only Current Field	Searches only the field in which the pointer is currently located, ignoring other fields in the table. When not selected, this option searches all fields for each record in the table. This option is on by default.	If you Search Only the Last Name field for "Smith," you would locate only those individuals whose last names are Smith. You would not locate anyone living in the town of Smith or on Smith Road.

To enter the zip code to find and the replacement zip code, and to search using the default options,

- Type **82891-**
- Press [Tab ↹].
- Type **828911605**
- Click [Find Next].

If necessary, move the dialog box so you can see the located entry.

Your screen should be similar to Figure 2-7.

field to search   located number

FIGURE 2-7

Date Hired	Last Name	First Name	Street	City	State	Zip Code	Phoi
1/12/90	Candelari	Richard	23 Mill Ave.	Tempe	AZ	86301-	(602)
2/20/90	Reynolds	Kimberly	8949 S. Summer St.	Tempe	AZ	86301-	(602)
3/5/90	Kennedy	James	5 E. Highland Rd.	Chandler	AZ	83174-2311	(602)
10/14/90	Anderson	Susan	4389 S. Hayden Rd.	Mesa	AZ	85205-0346	(602)
3/7/90	Falk	Nancy	470 S. Adams Rd.	Chandler	AZ	83174-	(602)
3/19/90	Dodd	Susan	23 Broadway Rd.	Mesa	AZ	84101-	(602)
4/12/91	Bergstrom	Drew	8943 W. Southern Ave.	Mesa	AZ	84101-8475	(602)
4/21/91	Steverson	Toni	76 Thomas Rd.	Phoenix	AZ	82891-	(602)
5/12/91	Camalette	Anthony	893 E. McDonald Rd.	Mesa	AZ	84101-	(602)

Replace in field: 'Zip Code'   ? ☒ 1268 (602)

text to locate ——

Find What: 82891-

Replace With: 828911605

Search: All

☐ Match Case
☑ Match Whole Field
☑ Search Only Current Field

Find Next
Replace
Replace All
Close

Record: 8 of 44

replacement   searches entire   modifies how search
text   table   is conducted

Immediately the highlight moves to the first occurrence of text in the document that matches the Find What text and highlights it. To replace the highlighted text,

■ Click Replace .

Access immediately continues searching and locates a second occurrence of the entry. You decide the program is locating the values accurately, and it will be safe to replace all finds with the replacement value. To do this,

■ Click Replace All .

When Access completes the search, the message "You won't be able to undo this Replace operation" is displayed. To approve the changes,

■ Click Yes .

It is much faster to use Replace All than to confirm each match separately. However, exercise care when using Replace All, because the search text you specify might be part of another word and you may accidentally replace text you want to keep.

■ In the same manner, update the zip code for 86301 to include the extension 1268.

■ Close the Replace in Field dialog box.

Over the past few days you have received several change request forms to update the employee records. The first change request is for Carman Artis, who recently married and has both a name and address change. To quickly locate this record you will use the Find command. This command works just like the Find and Replace command, except it does not enter a replacement.

- Move to the Last Name field of record 1.

- Click  Find.

- Type **artis**

- Click Find First.

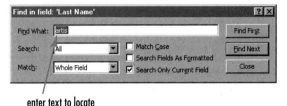

enter text to locate

The menu equivalent is **E**dit/**F**ind, and the keyboard shortcut is Ctrl + F.

Access searches the table and moves to the first occurrence of the entry. The Last Name field is highlighted in record 14. To change the last name to Richards,

- Close the dialog box.

- Type **Richards**

- Press ←Enter.

Because the Match Case option is not selected, Find will look for an exact match regardless of uppercase or lowercase characters.

Note: If the Find command did not locate this record, reissue the command and make sure you enter the name Artis exactly as shown and are searching the Last Name field.

Using Undo

Now that the highlight is on the First Name field, you notice this is the record for Jose Artis, not Carman. You changed the wrong record. You can use the Undo command to quickly undo this change.

You can use Undo to cancel your last action as long as you do not make any other changes to the table. Even if you save the record or the table, you can undo changes to the last edited record by using the Undo Saved Record command on the Edit menu or by clicking ⟲. Once you have changed another record or moved to another window, the earlier change cannot be undone. To quickly undo the change made to this record,

- Click ⟲ Undo.

You can also press Esc before leaving the field you are editing to cancel changes you have made.

The menu equivalent is **E**dit/**U**ndo, and the keyboard shortcut is Ctrl + Z.

Your screen should be similar to Figure 2-8.

Undo button   Find button

FIGURE 2-8

last name ——
change undone

Date Hired	Last Name	First Name	Street	City	State	Zip Code	Pho
8/14/91	Artis	Jose	358 Maple Dr.	Scottsdale	AZ	85205-6911	(602)
10/10/91	Spehr	Timothy	90 E. Royal Dr.	Chandler	AZ	83174-	(602)
10/14/90	Anderson	Susan	4389 S. Hayden Rd.	Mesa	AZ	85205-0346	(602)
1/7/92	Williamson	Anthony	89 College Ave.	Mesa	AZ	84101-0785	(602)
2/1/92	Little	Jennifer	987 Campus Dr.	Scottsdale	AZ	85201-6760	(602)
3/4/92	Rawitzer	Kevin	23 Mill Ave.	Tempe	AZ	86301-1268	(602)
11/5/92	DeLuca	Elizabeth	21 W. Southern Ave.	Mesa	AZ	84101-1169	(602)
11/7/92	Thorp	Blake	87 E. Aurora Ave.	Scottsdale	AZ	85205-6890	(602)
12/1/92	Fadaro	Jane	89 S. Central Ave.	Phoenix	AZ	82891-1605	(602)
6/9/93	Ramage	Meg	90 E. Rawhide Ave.	Scottsdale	AZ	85205-7582	(602)
7/8/93	Fulton	Cindy	75 Brooklea Dr.	Scottsdale	AZ	85205-5829	(602)

The original field value of "Artis" replaces "Richards."

■ To continue the search to locate the next record with the last name of Artis, move back to the Last Name field of this record.

■ Click 🔍 Find.

■ Click **Find Next** .

■ Close the Find in Field dialog box.

■ Change the last name to **Richards** and the street to **5401 E. Thomas Rd.**

■ Use the Find command to search the table for the following records and correct the entries.

Reminder: The insertion point must be on the field you want to search before clicking 🔍 Find.

Employee Name	Field	Correction
Adam Robson	Street	**4290 E. Alameda Dr.**
Kevin Hanson	City, Zip Code	**Scottsdale, 85205-3211**
Meg Ramage	Last Name	**Miller**

■ When you are done, return to the first field of record 1.

Inserting a Field

While continuing to use the table, you have realized that you need to include a field of information to hold each employee's gender. Although it is better to include all the necessary fields when creating the table structure, it is possible to add or remove fields from a table at a later time. After looking at the order of the

fields, you decide to add the new field, Gender, between the Phone Number and
Birth Date fields. To insert the new field in the table and define its properties,

- Click 📝 Design View.

- Make the Birth Date field current.

- Click ⬛ Insert Rows.

- Enter the new field information as follows:

Field Name:	**Gender**
Data Type:	**Text**
Description:	**Enter M for male or F for female.**
Field Size:	**1**
Format:	**>**

Your screen should be similar to Figure 2-9.

If you remove a field, Access permanently
deletes the field definition and any data in
the field. ⬛ or **E**dit/Delete **R**ow removes
a field.

You can also add or delete fields in
Datasheet view.

The menu equivalent is **I**nsert/**F**ield. You
can also use the Insert Field command on
the Shortcut menu.

new field ⟶   Insert Rows button ⟶   ⟵ Delete Rows button

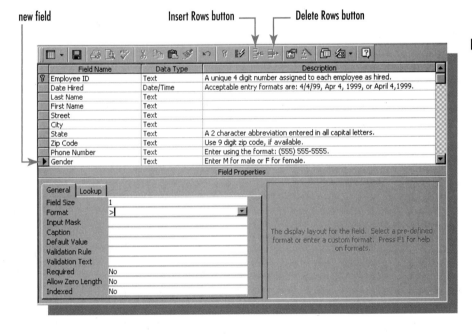

FIGURE 2-9

Adding Validity Checks

The only two characters you want the Gender field to accept are M for male and
F for female. To specify that these two characters are the only entries acceptable
in the field, you will include a validity check.

Concept 5: Validity Checks

Access automatically performs certain checks, called **validity checks**, on values entered in a field to make sure that the values are valid for the field type. A Text field type has few restrictions, but you can create your own validity checks for a field, which Access will apply during data entry.

A validity check is set by entering an expression to describe acceptable values. **Expressions** are combinations of symbols that produce specific results. Expressions are used throughout Access to create validity checks, queries, forms, and reports. These are examples of possible expressions:

Expression	Result
=[Sales Amount] + [Sales Tax]	Sums value in two fields
="M" OR "F"	Includes M or F entries only
>=#1/1/95# AND <=#12/31/95#	Includes entries greater than or equal to 1/1/95, and less than or equal to 12/31/95
="Tennis Rackets"	Includes Tennis Rackets entries only

You create an expression by combining identifiers, operators, and values to produce the desired result. An **identifier** is an element that refers to the value of a field, a graphical object, or property. In the expression =[Sales Amount] + [Sales Tax], [Sales Amount] and [Sales Tax] are identifiers that refer to the values in the Sales Amount and Sales Tax fields.

An **operator** is a symbol or word that indicates that an operation is to be performed. The Access operators include = (equal to), <> (not equal to), >= (greater than or equal to), <= (less than or equal to), LIKE, OR, and AND. In the expression ="M" OR "F", the = sign and OR are operators. The = operator is assumed if no other operator is specified.

Values are numbers, dates, or groups of characters. Character strings such as "M", "F", or "Tennis Rackets"are enclosed in quotation marks. Dates are enclosed in pound signs (#), as in >=#1/1/95# AND <=#12/31/95#.

When you add a validity check, you can also add validation text in the Validation Text property box. **Validation text** appears in a message box if you attempt to enter invalid information in a text field for which there is a validity check. For example, if you added a validity check to a field to only allow the numbers 1 through 10, you might create validation text that would display the message, "The only valid entries for this field are numbers 1 through 10." If you do not specify a message, Access displays a default error message, which will not clearly describe the reason for the error.

You want to add a validity check to allow only M or F to be entered in the field. You also want to include a Validation Text message that will be displayed if the wrong character is entered in the Gender field.

- ■ Move to the Validation Rule field property text box.

- ■ Type =**M or F**

- ■ Press ⏎Enter.

- ■ Type **The only valid entries are M or F**

Your screen should be similar to Figure 2-10.

current field

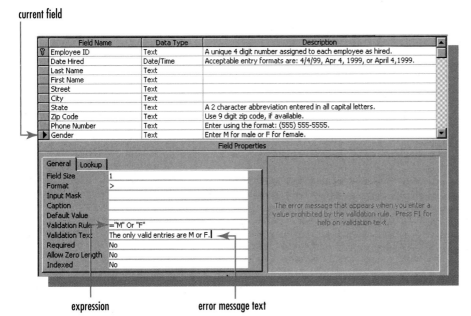

FIGURE 2-10

expression   error message text

The expression states that the acceptable values can only be equal to an M or an F. Notice that Access automatically added quotation marks around the two character strings and changed the "o" in "or" to uppercase.

Next you want to add the data for the Gender field to the table.

Because the Format property has been set to convert all entries to uppercase, an entry of m or f is also acceptable.

■ Click 🏢 Datasheet.

■ Click 〔 Yes 〕.

A message box appears advising you that data integrity rules have been changed. When you restructure a table, you often make changes that could result in a loss of data. Changes such as shortening field sizes, creating validity checks, or changing field types can cause existing data to become invalid. Because the field is new, there are no data values to verify, and a validation check is unnecessary. To continue,

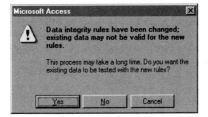

■ Choose 〔 No 〕.

■ Move to the Gender field for record 1.

Your screen should be similar to Figure 2-11.

new field

FIGURE 2-11

Street	City	State	Zip Code	Phone Number	Gender	Birth Date
23 Mill Ave.	Tempe	AZ	86301-1268	(602) 555-3333		7/7/6
8949 S. Summer St.	Tempe	AZ	86301-1268	(602) 555-4000		1/4/5
5 E. Highland Rd.	Chandler	AZ	83174-2311	(602) 555-5566		10/7/6
4389 S. Hayden Rd.	Mesa	AZ	85205-0346	(602) 555-1950		6/14/6
470 S. Adams Rd.	Chandler	AZ	83174-	(602) 555-7380		4/11/6
23 Broadway Rd.	Mesa	AZ	84101-	(602) 939-3333		8/8/6
8943 W. Southern Ave.	Mesa	AZ	84101-8475	(602) 555-8201		8/7/6
76 Thomas Rd.	Phoenix	AZ	82891-1605	(602) 555-2222		8/1/6
893 E. McDonald Rd.	Mesa	AZ	84101-	(602) 555-7830		8/9/7

The new field was added to the table between the Phone Number and Birth Date fields.

Hiding and Redisplaying Fields

You can most likely tell the gender for each record by looking at the employee's first name. Unfortunately, you cannot see the First Name field at the same time you are entering data in the Gender field. A quick way to view the fields side by side is to hide the fields that are in between.

> **Drag in the column heads to select the fields.**

- Select the Street field through the Phone Number field.
- Choose Format/Hide Columns.

Now both the First Name and Gender columns are next to each other, and you can see the first name for record 1 is Richard. Therefore the Gender field for record 1 should be M. To verify that the validity check works, you will enter an invalid field value in the Gender field for this record.

- Type **g**
- Press ←Enter.

Your screen should be similar to Figure 2-12.

Street field through Phone
Number field hidden   invalid entry

FIGURE 2-12

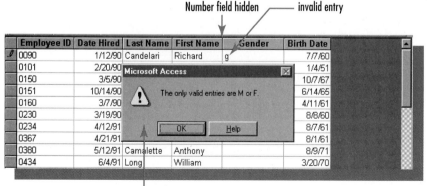

error message box

Access displays the error message you entered in the Validation Text box of the Design view. To clear the error message and correct the entry,

- Click [OK].

- Press [←Backspace].

- Type **m**

- Press [↓].

The entry for the first record is displayed as an uppercase M. Next you will enter the gender for each record and then redisplay the hidden fields.

- Enter the Gender field values for the remaining records by looking at the First Name field to determine whether the employee is male or female.

- Reduce the size of the Gender field using the Best Fit command.

- Choose F**o**rmat/**U**nhide Columns.

- Select the five fields that do not display checkmarks.

- Click [Close].

- Move to the first field of record 1.

hidden fields are not selected

Sorting on a Single Field

As you may recall from Lab 1, the records are ordered by the primary key field, Employee ID. The Accounting department manager, however, has asked you for an alphabetical list of all employees. To do this you can sort the records in the table.

Concept 6: Sort

You can quickly reorder records in a table by **sorting** a table to display in a different record order. Sorting data often helps you find specific information quickly. In Access you can sort data in ascending order (A to Z or 0 to 9) or descending order (Z to A or 9 to 0).

You can sort all records in a table by a single field, such as State, or you can select adjacent columns and sort by more than one field, such as State and then City. When you select multiple columns to sort, Access sorts records starting with the column farthest left, then moves to the right across the columns. For example, if you want to quickly sort by State, then by City, the State field must be to the left of the City field.

Access saves the new sort order with your table data and reapplies it automatically each time you open the table. To return to the primary key sort order, you must remove the temporary sort.

For the first sort, you want the records arranged in ascending alphabetical order by last name.

- Move to the Last Name field of any record.

- Click [A↓] Sort Ascending.

The menu equivalent is **R**ecords/**S**ort/**A**scending.

DATABASE

Your screen should be similar to Figure 2-13.

Sort Ascending
button   Sort Descending button

FIGURE 2-13

Employee ID	Date Hired	Last Name	First Name	Street	City	State	Z
▶ 3550	11/15/95	Adams	Thomas	1324 S. Price Rd.	Tempe	AZ	86
0151	10/14/90	Anderson	Susan	4389 S. Hayden Rd.	Mesa	AZ	85
1151	10/14/90	Anderson	Susan	4389 S. Hayden Rd.	Mesa	AZ	85
0839	8/14/91	Artis	Jose	358 Maple Dr.	Scottsdale	AZ	85
0234	4/12/91	Bergstrom	Drew	8943 W. Southern Ave.	Mesa	AZ	84
3501	9/4/94	Briggs	Scott	45 E. Camelback Rd.	Phoenix	AZ	82
2312	11/4/93	Broeker	Kimberly	23 Price Rd.	Tempe	AZ	86
2341	2/4/94	Cady	Helen	34 University Dr.	Tempe	AZ	85
0380	5/12/91	Camalette	Anthony	893 E. McDonald Rd.	Mesa	AZ	84
0090	1/12/90	Candelari	Richard	23 Mill Ave.	Tempe	AZ	86
1460	11/5/92	DeLuca	Elizabeth	21 W. Southern Ave.	Mesa	AZ	84
0230	3/19/90	Dodd	Susan	23 Broadway Rd.	Mesa	AZ	84
3490	3/4/94	Dunn	William	947 S. Forest St.	Tempe	AZ	86
3389	3/4/94	Ehmann	Kurt	7867 Forest Ave.	Phoenix	AZ	82
1481	12/1/92	Fadaro	Jane	89 S. Central Ave.	Phoenix	AZ	82
0160	3/7/90	Falk	Nancy	470 S. Adams Rd.	Chandler	AZ	83
1560	7/8/93	Fulton	Cindy	75 Brooklea Dr.	Scottsdale	AZ	85
3554	11/15/95	Granger	Michael	12 E. 7th St.	Phoenix	AZ	82

Record: |◄ ◄ | 1 | ► ►| ►* | of 44

duplicate records ←

records sorted by last name

The employee records are displayed in alphabetical order by last name.

Deleting Records

Now that the records are alphabetically arranged, you immediately notice that Susan Anderson's record has been entered into the table twice. The records contain identical information in all the fields except for the Employee ID field. By checking the employee card, you determine that the record with the employee number of 1151 is incorrect. You need to delete the duplicate record.

Records can be removed from a table by selecting the entire record and pressing Delete or clicking 🗡 Cut. This method is useful when you have multiple records to be deleted that you can select and delete as a group. It is quicker, however, to use the ✂ Delete Record button when you want to remove records individually. This is because the record is both selected and deleted at the same time.

> You cannot use Undo to restore deleted records.

> Records are selected using **E**dit/Se**l**ect Record or by clicking in the row selector when the mouse pointer shape is ➡. In Navigation mode ⇧Shift+Spacebar selects the current record.

> The menu equivalent is **E**dit/Cu**t**, and the keyboard shortcut is Ctrl + X. The Cut command is also on the Shortcut menu when a record is selected.

■ Move to any field in record 3.

■ Click ✂ Delete Record.

As a precaution against accidentally deleting records, Access displays a confirmation dialog box. To indicate you want to permanently delete the record,

■ Click  .

Microsoft Access	✕
⚠ **You are about to delete 1 record(s).**
If you click Yes, you won't be able to undo this Delete operation. Are you sure you want to delete these records?
[Yes]   [No]

Your screen should be similar to Figure 2-14.

deletes selected record

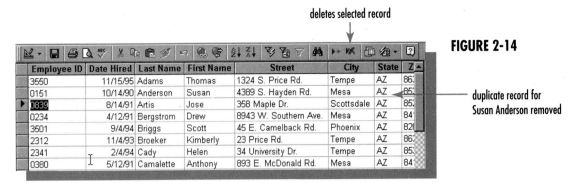

FIGURE 2-14

duplicate record for
Susan Anderson removed

Sorting on Multiple Fields

■ Use the scroll box to scroll down to record 27.

Notice that the records for Patty and Carman Richards are sorted by last name but not by first name. You want the records that have the same last name to be further sorted by first name. To do this, you specify multiple sort fields. When sorting on multiple fields, the fields must be adjacent to each other, and the most important field in the sort must be to the left of the secondary field. The Last Name and First Name fields are already in the correct locations for the sort you want to perform. To specify the fields to sort on, both columns must be selected.

■ Select the Last Name and First Name field columns.

■ Click [A↓] Sort Ascending.

■ Scroll down to record 27 again.

Your screen should be similar to Figure 2-15.

> As you drag the scroll box, the record location is displayed in the scroll tips box.
>
> Record: 27 of 43

> If the columns are not adjacent, you can hide the columns that are in between. If they are not in the correct order, you can move the columns. You will learn how to do this in Lab 3.

records sorted by last name and first name

Employee ID	Date Hired	Last Name	First Name	Street	City	State	Z
0600	6/10/91	Reynolds	Cara	832 S. William Ave.	Tempe	AZ	86:
0101	2/20/90	Reynolds	Kimberly	8949 S. Summer St.	Tempe	AZ	86:
2300	8/16/93	Richards	Carman	5401 E. Thomas Rd.	Mesa	AZ	84:
3561	11/21/95	Richards	Patty	345 W. Mill Ave.	Mesa	AZ	84:
2340	1/5/94	Robson	Adam	4290 E. Alameda Dr.	Scottsdale	AZ	85:
3800	12/8/95	Samuals	Scott	90 First Ave.	Phoenix	AZ	82(
2321	12/1/93	Shearing	Cory	235 N. Cactus Dr.	Scottsdale	AZ	85:
2315	11/4/93	Smalley	Jill	984 W. Thomas Rd.	Phoenix	AZ	82(
2322	12/1/93	Smith	Bonnie	564 S. Lemon Dr.	Mesa	AZ	84:

FIGURE 2-15

As you can see, sorting is a fast, useful tool. The sort order remains in effect until you remove the sort or replace it with a new sort order. Although Access remembers your sort order even when you exit the program, it does not actually change the table records. You can remove the sort at any time to restore the records to the primary key sort order. To do this,

- ■ Choose **R**ecords/**R**emove Filter/Sort.

- ■ Close the table and save your design changes.

Note: If you are ending your session now, close the database file and exit Access. When you begin Part 2, load Access and open the Employee Records file.

Part 2

Creating a Form

One of your responsibilities is to make the database easy to use. You know from experience that long hours of viewing large tables can be tiring. Therefore you want to create an onscreen form to make this table easier to view and use.

Concept 7: Forms

Forms are database objects used primarily to display records onscreen to make it easier to enter new records and to make changes to existing records. Forms are based on an underlying table and include design elements such as descriptive text, titles, labels, lines, boxes, and pictures. Forms often use calculations as well, to summarize data that is not listed on the actual table, such as a sales total. Forms make working with long lists of data easier. They enable people to use the data in the tables without having to sift through many lines of data to find the exact record.

Forms are linked to the underlying table by using controls. **Controls** are graphical objects that can be selected and modified. Once a control is selected, it can be sized, moved, or enhanced in other ways. The most common type of control is a text box. A **text box control** creates a link to the underlying source, usually a field from a table, and displays the field entry in the form. This type of control is called a **bound control** because it is tied to a field in an underlying table. The form usually also includes a label with each text box control. A **label control** initially displays the field name from the underlying table associated with the text box control. Label controls can also display custom names you want to display instead of the field name or other descriptive text entries such as a title or instructions for the user. These controls are **unbound controls** because they are not connected to a field. Other unbound controls contain elements that enhance the appearance of the form such as lines, boxes, and pictures. A third type of control is a **calculated control** that displays the results of a calculation in the form. It uses an expression that uses data from the underlying table or another control as its source of data.

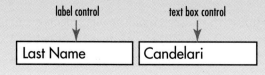

You will create a form to be used by the Personnel department to add new employee records and to update existing employee records in the Sports Company Employees table. The input for the table comes from the paper Employee Data form that each employee fills out when hired. The paper form looks like this:

EMPLOYEE DATA

First Name: _____   Last Name: _____

Street: _____

City: _____   State: _____   Zip Code: _____

Phone Number: _____

Gender: _____   Birth Date: _____

For Personnel Use Only:

Employee ID: _____
Date Hired: _____

The order of information in the Employee Data form is different than the order that the data is entered into the table. To make the job of data entry easier, you want the table form to reflect the order of the paper form used by employees. As when creating a table, there are several different methods that can be used to create a form. You will use the Form Wizard to guide you through the steps to create a form.

- ■ To create a form, open the Forms tab.

- ■ Click [New].

- ■ Select Form Wizard.

- ■ Click [OK].

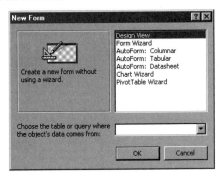

The first Form Wizard dialog box on your screen should be similar to Figure 2-16.

FIGURE 2-16

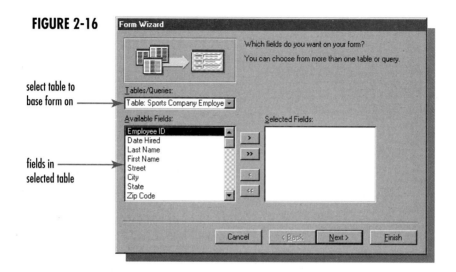

select table to
base form on

fields in
selected table

The dialog box displays the name of the current table, Sports Company Employees, in the Tables/Queries list box. This is the table that Access will use when creating the form. If your database contained multiple tables, you would display the Tables/Queries drop-down list to select a different table.

After selecting the table, you select the fields to include in the form. The fields from the selected table will appear in the Available Fields list box. The order in which you select the fields is the **tab order**, or the order in which the highlight will move through the fields on the form during data entry. You would like the order to be the same as the order on the paper form. To add the First Name field to the form first, from the Available Fields list box,

> You can also double-click on each field name in the Available Fields list box to move the field name to the Selected Fields list box.

> The ▶▶ button adds all available fields to the Selected Fields list.

■ Select First Name.

■ Click ▶.

The First Name field is removed from the Available Fields list and added to the top of the Selected Fields list box.

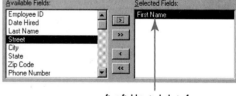

first field to include in form

■ In the same manner, select the fields in the order shown below and add them to the Selected Fields list.

Last Name
Street
City
State
Zip Code
Phone Number
Gender
Birth Date
Employee ID
Date Hired

When you are done, the Available Fields list box should be empty, and the Selected Fields list box should list the fields in the selected order. To move to the next Form Wizard screen,

fields in selected order

■ Click ⌈ Next > ⌉.

The second Form Wizard dialog box on your screen should be similar to Figure 2-17.

four form layouts

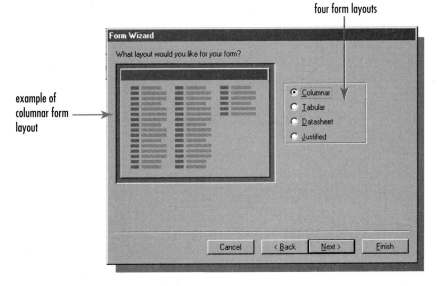

example of columnar form layout

FIGURE 2-17

In this dialog box you are asked to select the layout for the form. Four form layouts are available: Columnar, Tabular, Datasheet and Justified. They are described in the table below.

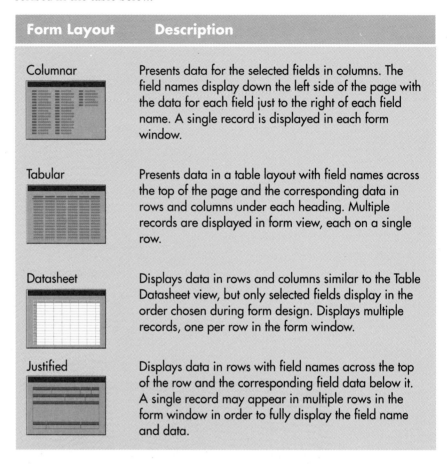

Form Layout	Description
Columnar	Presents data for the selected fields in columns. The field names display down the left side of the page with the data for each field just to the right of each field name. A single record is displayed in each form window.
Tabular	Presents data in a table layout with field names across the top of the page and the corresponding data in rows and columns under each heading. Multiple records are displayed in form view, each on a single row.
Datasheet	Displays data in rows and columns similar to the Table Datasheet view, but only selected fields display in the order chosen during form design. Displays multiple records, one per row in the form window.
Justified	Displays data in rows with field names across the top of the row and the corresponding field data below it. A single record may appear in multiple rows in the form window in order to fully display the field name and data.

The columnar layout would appear most similar to the paper form currently in use by the personnel department.

■   If necessary, select Columnar.

■   Click   Next >   .

From the next dialog box you select from ten different styles for your form. A sample of each style as it is selected is displayed on the left side of the dialog box. You will create the form using the Clouds style.

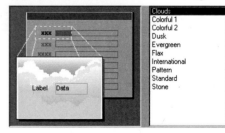

■   Select Clouds.

■   Click   Next >   .

Finally, you need to enter a form title to be used as the name of the form and to specify whether the form should open with data displayed in it. You want the form to display data, but you want to change the form's title. To do this,

- ■   Type **Employee Data Form**

- ■   Click ▢ Finish ▢.

The Wizard uses the name of the table as the default form title.

The completed form is displayed in the Form view window. This view typically displays one record at a time in the form for data entry or editing purposes.

- ■   If necessary, maximize the Form window.

Your screen should be similar to Figure 2-18.

field label displays   text box displays data
field name

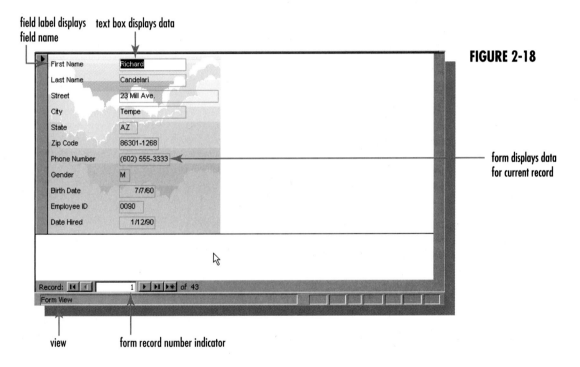

FIGURE 2-18

form displays data
for current record

view   form record number indicator

The form displays the selected fields in columnar layout using the Clouds style. The field name labels are in a column along the left margin, and the field text boxes are in an adjacent column to the right. The employee information for Richard Candelari, record number 1, is displayed in the text boxes.

You use the same navigation keys in Form view that you used in Datasheet view. You can move between fields in the form by using the navigation buttons at the bottom of the form, or the [Tab⇆], [←Enter], [⇧Shift] +[Tab⇆], and directional arrow keys on the keyboard. In addition, the [Page Up] and [Page Down] keys allow you to move between records in Form view.

- ■   Move to record 2.

Kimberly Reynolds' record is displayed in the form.

Now that you have looked at the first two records, you want to change the layout of the form to more closely resemble the paper entry form used in the Personnel department. Form Design view is used to design a new form or to change the layout of an existing form.

The menu equivalent is **V**iew/**D**esign View.

■ Click  Design View.

Your screen should be similar to Figure 2-19.

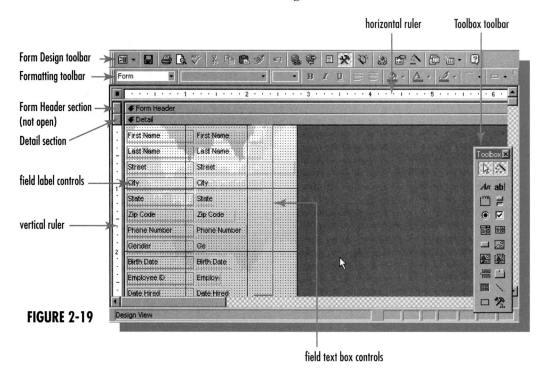

FIGURE 2-19

field text box controls

Form Design view displays the form in a window that is bordered along the top by a horizontal ruler and along the left by a vertical ruler. The rulers help you correctly place items in the Form Design window.

The Form Design view automatically displays three toolbars: Form Design, Formatting, and Toolbox. The Form Design toolbar contains the standard buttons as well as buttons that are specific to the Form Design view window. These buttons are identified below.

The Formatting toolbar contains buttons that allow you to make text enhancements. The buttons on the Formatting toolbar are identified below.

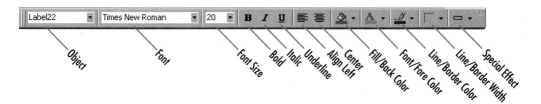

The Toolbox toolbar contains buttons that are used to add and modify controls. The Toolbox buttons are identified below.

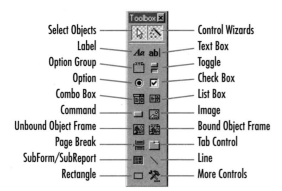

> If the Toolbox is not displayed, click [⚒] Toolbox on the Form Design toolbar.

> The Toolbox on your screen may be in a different location than in Figure 2-19. If necessary, move the Toolbox to the bottom right corner of the window.

The Form Design window is divided into three areas, Form Header, Detail, and Form Footer (see Figure 2-19). The contents of each section appear below the horizontal bar containing the name. The sections are described in the table below.

Section	Description
Form Header	An optional section that you can include to display information such as the form title, instructions, or graphics. The contents of a Form Header appear at the top of the screen or, if you print the form, at the top of the first page. Form Headers are not visible in Datasheet view, and do not scroll as you scroll through records. The Form Header currently contains no data.
Detail	The area where the table data displays. The Detail section currently displays the controls for the Sports Company Employees table.
Form Footer	Another optional section that can include notes, instructions, or grand totals. Form Footers appear at the bottom of the screen or, if printed, at the end of the last page. Like Form Headers, Form Footers do not display in Datasheet view. The Form Footer section currently contains no data.

> If necessary, scroll down to view the Form Footer section.

Selecting Controls

Every object in a form is contained in a control. In this form design, the label controls are to the left of the text box controls. You need to select controls in the form to modify them. To select the First Name control,

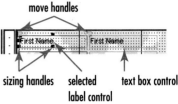

> *Remember that the label controls are on the left in each set of controls.*

> *The mouse pointer must be ₨ when selecting controls.*

■ Click First Name label control.

The First Name label control is surrounded by eight small boxes, called **sizing handles**, that indicate the label control is selected. The sizing handles are used to size the control. In addition a large box in the upper left corner is displayed. This is a **move handle** that is used to move the selected control. Notice the text box control also displays a move handle. This indicates that the two controls will act as one when manipulated. This type of control is called a **compound control**.

■ Click First Name text box control.

> *You can also press [Tab ⇥] to select the next control. [⇧Shift]+[Tab ⇥] selects the previous control.*

Now the text box control is surrounded by eight sizing handles, indicating that it is the selected control. The move handle still appears on both parts of the compound control.

Moving and Sizing Controls

Once you select a control, you can change its location and size. The grid of dots helps you position the controls on the form. It not only provides a visual guide to positioning and sizing controls, but controls are "snapped" to the grid, or automatically positioned on the nearest grid line. You will rearrange the controls in the form as shown in Figure 2-20 on the next page.

> *You can also delete controls by selecting them, then pressing [Delete].*

> *When you first click on a control, the 🖑 shape appears and will display as long as you hold down the mouse button.*

> *Do not point to a sizing or move handle.*

> *The move handle is used to move just the text box or label control independently in a compound control.*

You will begin by moving the Last Name label and text box controls to begin at the 2.5-inch position on the same line. When you can move a selected control, the mouse pointer shape appears as 🖑. You can then drag the control to any location in the form. As you move the controls, the right edge of the form will expand to accommodate the new width of the design.

> *You can also move controls using [Ctrl]+ the directional arrow keys.*

■ Select either part of the Last Name compound control.

■ Point to the top or bottom border of the control.

■ When the mouse pointer is a 🖑, drag the control to the right until the left edge of the outline aligns with the 2.5-inch ruler position.

■ Next, drag the First Name controls down the left margin of the form to the same line as the Last Name.

■ In a similar manner, move the other controls to the positions shown in Figure 2-20.

Do not be concerned if your controls are not evenly aligned with the left edge of the form or on the lines. You will learn how to adjust the spacing next.

Your screen should be similar to Figure 2-20.

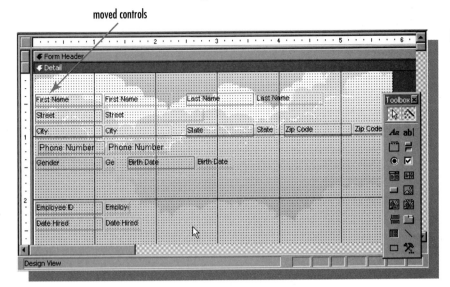

FIGURE 2-20

Next you will increase the size of the Street text box control. When you position the mouse pointer on a sizing handle, it changes to a ⟷. The direction of the arrow indicates in which direction dragging the mouse will alter the shape of the object. This is similar to sizing a window.

- Select the Street text box control.

- Point to the middle handle on the right end of the Street text box control.

- When the mouse pointer appears as ⟷, drag the control to the right until it aligns with the end of the Last Name text box control on the line above it.

Aligning Controls

Next you need to align the First Name, Street, City, Phone Number, and Gender controls to ensure that they are even along the left edge. Rather than selecting each control individually and moving it, you can select several controls at the same time. When you select multiple controls, you can move all the selected controls as a group, align the selected controls so they are evenly spaced or in line one below the other, or make other changes to the entire group of controls. To select multiple controls hold down ⇧Shift while clicking on each control. To select, then align these controls as a group,

- Hold down ⇧Shift.
- Click the First Name, Street, City, Phone Number, and Gender controls.
- Release ⇧Shift.
- Choose Format/Align/Left.
- Deselect the controls by clicking any blank area of the form.

When aligning controls, select only controls that are in the same row or column.

DATABASE

Your screen should be similar to Figure 2-21.

FIGURE 2-21

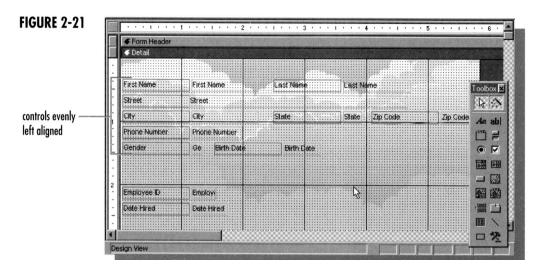

controls evenly
left aligned

The controls all shifted to the left and are aligned with the control that was farthest left. You now want to adjust the spacing between all the controls in the upper section of this form to ensure that there is an even amount of vertical space between each control. This vertical spacing can be adjusted between any group of selected controls.

Another way to select controls is to drag a selection box around the controls. To select the controls using this method, point to a blank area above the first control and drag until the box surrounds the controls you want to select. When you release the mouse button, all the controls inside the box will be selected. To make the vertical spacing equal between these controls,

- Select all the controls (excluding the Employee ID and Date Hired controls) on the form by dragging a selection box around them.

- Choose Format/Vertical Spacing/Make Equal.

- Deselect the controls.

The vertical space between controls is adjusted to make the vertical spacing between the selected controls equal. The top and bottom controls do not change locations; only the middle controls in the selection are adjusted to equalize the spacing.

> You can fine-tune placement by selecting a control and using Ctrl + directional keys to move it in increments.

> At least three controls must be selected, and if they are compound controls, the text box part of the control must be selected.

Adding Text to a Form

Next you will add a label control in the form header to display the form title. In addition, you want to add two subheads within the form to identify the personal data and company data areas. The Toolbox buttons let you add text, arrows, boxes, and other design elements to a form. To add the control to the form header, you first need to add a space in the Form Header area.

■ Point to the top of the Detail section bar.

■ When the mouse pointer is a ✛, drag the Detail section bar down approximately 1/2-inch on the vertical ruler.

Your screen should be similar to Figure 2-22.

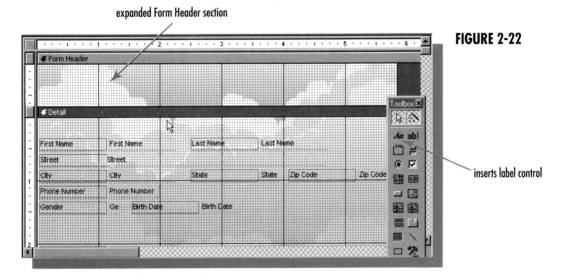

expanded Form Header section

FIGURE 2-22

inserts label control

The ▣ on the Toolbox is used to add a label control to a form. The mouse pointer changes to $+_A$ when this feature is in use. You indicate where you want the control to appear by clicking on the location in the window. Then an insertion point is displayed indicating that you can begin typing the descriptive label.

■ Click ▣ Label

■ Click in the Form Header area.

■ Type **The Sports Company Employee Record**

■ Press ⏎Enter.

> You can edit text in label controls just as you edit other text.

The text entry feature is turned off. The form title appears in a label control box and can be sized and moved like any other control. Now you will add two more label controls for the subheads in the Detail section.

- ■ Click **Aa** Label.

- ■ Click in the space above the First Name control in the Detail section.

- ■ Type **Personal Data:**

- ■ Press. ⏎Enter.

- ■ In a similar manner, enter the subhead **Company Data:** in the space above the Employee ID control.

Your screen should be similar to Figure 2-23.

form header label control

FIGURE 2-23

label controls

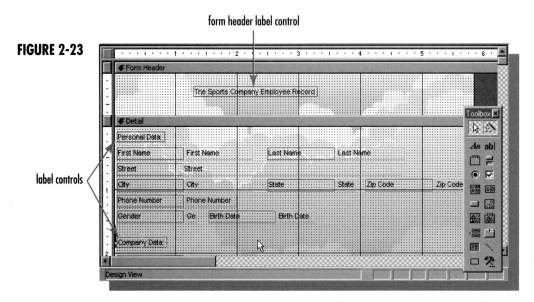

- ■ Align the two subhead label controls along the left edge and adjust their vertical spacing appropriately.

Changing Fonts

You can further change the way a form appears by changing the font settings of the text in the controls.

Concept 8: Fonts

Fonts consist of three elements: typeface, size, and style that can be applied to characters to improve their appearance. A **typeface** is the design and shape of characters. Two common typefaces are Times New Roman and Courier. Type size refers to the size of the printed characters and is commonly measured in **points**. A 72-point character is 1 inch tall. The most common type size for text is 10 or 12 points.

Type style refers to the special attributes you assign to characters, such as bold or italic. You can also add special effects such as underlines and color to the characters.

Several common fonts in different sizes and styles are shown in the table below.

Font Name	Font Size	Font Style
Arial	This is 12 pt. This is 18 pt.	**Bold 18 pt.**
Courier New	This is 12 pt. This is 18 pt.	**Bold 18 pt.**
Times New Roman	This is 12 pt. This is 18 pt.	**Bold 18 pt.**

Although you must apply font changes to entire controls rather than changing individual characters or words, you can apply multiple font changes to a table, form, or report by selecting and changing fonts for individual controls. You should be careful, however, not to combine too many different fonts and colors or to use fancy fonts that might make it difficult to read the screen or are distracting to use for long periods of time.

The first text enhancement you want to make is to increase the font size of the text in all controls of the form. Larger fonts make it easier to read the data that is displayed in the form.

■ Choose Edit/Select All.

The keyboard shortcut in Ctrl +A.

The Formatting toolbar buttons are used to make text enhancements, such as changing the font, font size, font style, or adding color. Notice that the Font

Size button displays "8" as the point size of all text in the selected controls. You want to increase the font size to 10 points.

■ Open the Font Size [8 ▾] drop-down list and select 10.

The point size of all text in the selected controls changes to 10 points and is now much easier to read. Next you want to make the form title an even larger font size. You also want to change the title typeface from the default typeface of Arial to Times New Roman.

■ Select the form header label control.

■ Open the Font [Arial ▾] drop-down list and select Times New Roman as the typeface.

■ Change the form header font size to 20.

Now the title is too large to be fully displayed in the control box. You can size the control to fully display the label by dragging on the selection handles as you did earlier, or you can allow Access to automatically size the control to fit the contents. To automatically resize the control,

■ Choose F**o**rmat/**S**ize/T**o** **F**it.

■ Move the form header label control to center it in the Form Header section.

Your screen should be similar to Figure 2-24.

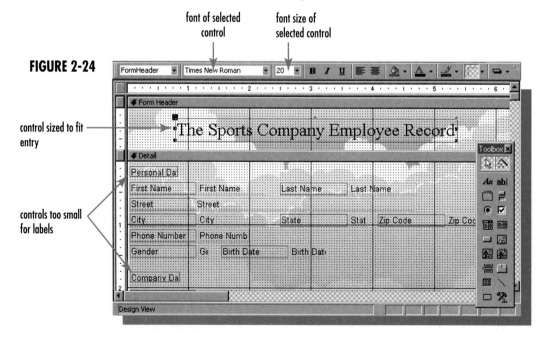

FIGURE 2-24

font of selected control

font size of selected control

control sized to fit entry

controls too small for labels

You also want to size the controls of the subheads and change their labels to bold to make them stand out from the rest of the text.

- ■ Select the Personal Data label control.
- ■ Click **B** Bold.
- ■ Choose Format/Size/To Fit.
- ■ In a similar manner, bold and size the Company Data label control.
- ■ If necessary, adjust the vertical spacing of the two label controls.

Adding Text Color

You can also make controls more noticeable by adding color to their background, text, or borders. In addition, you can use special effects such as shadows to enhance the control border. You will make the text in the form header label red and add a shadow box to the control.

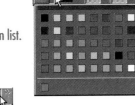

- ■ Select the form header label control.
- ■ Open the  Font/Fore Color drop-down list.
- ■ Click ■ (red).
- ■ Open the ▭ Special Effects drop-down list.
- ■ Click ▭ Shadowed.
- ■ Clear the selection.

The color and shadow settings have been applied to the form title. To see how the form will look onscreen, you will switch to Form view.

- ■ Click 🖽 Form View.

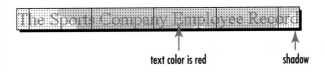

text color is red · · · · · shadow

The menu equivalent is **V**iew/**F**orm View.

DATABASE

Your screen should be similar to Figure 2-25.

FIGURE 2-25

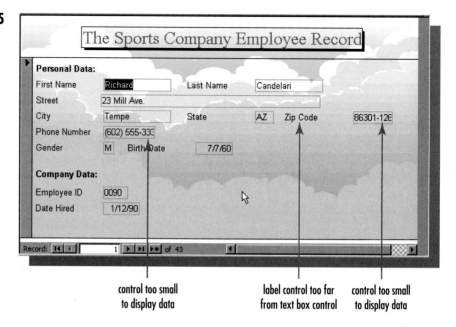

control too small   label control too far   control too small
to display data   from text box control   to display data

The layout and design changes greatly enhance the appearance of the form. However, now you can also see that the Zip Code and Phone Number text box controls are not wide enough to display the data in the fields. You also notice that some of the text box controls are separated by too much space from the label controls. You will increase the size of the label controls and move the text box controls closer to their labels to decrease the space between the label and data.

> Depending on your screen display, other controls may not be wide enough. Make the necessary adjustments as you did for the Zip Code and Phone Number fields.

■ Switch back to Form Design view.

■ Increase the size of the Zip Code and Phone Number text box controls.

■ Reduce the size of the State, Zip Code, and Birth Date label controls.

■ Select the State text box control.

■ Point to the move handle of the State text box control.

■ When the mouse pointer is a 👆, drag the control closer to the State label control.

■ In a similar manner, adjust the Zip Code and Birth Date text box controls.

■ Return to Form view.

Your screen should be similar to Figure 2-26.

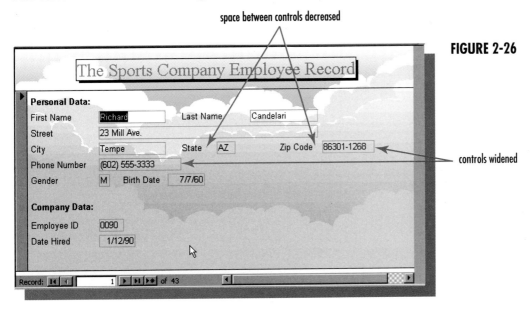

FIGURE 2-26

Entering Records in Form View

Now that the custom form is complete, you can use it to enter new records.

■ Move to a new blank entry form and enter the following data for a new record.

EMPLOYEE DATA

First Name: **Brent**   Last Name: **Smith**

Street: **89 E. Southern Dr.**

City: **Tempe**   State: **AZ**   Zip Code: **85301-2316**

Phone Number: **(606) 555-1234**

Gender: **M**   Birth Date: **April 13, 1971**

For Personnel Use Only:

Employee ID: **1027**
Date Hired: **September 12, 1995**

Use ▶* New Record in the Form toolbar or the ▶* navigation button to display a blank form.

Press [Tab ⇥] to move to the next control.

The input masks will appear in the form as you type in the field's control.

Using the form makes entering the new employee data much faster because the fields are in the same order as the information in the paper Employee Data form used by the Personnel department.

■ Enter another record using your special Employee ID 9999 and your first and last name. The data in all other fields can be fictitious, except enter the current date as your date hired.

The menu equivalent is **V**iew/Data**s**heet View.

■ To see the records you entered in Form Datasheet view, open the [🖩▾] View button drop-down list and click [▥] Datasheet view.

■ Scroll up a few rows to display both new records.

Your screen should be similar to Figure 2-27.

field order same as on form

FIGURE 2-27

First Name	Last Name	Street	City	Sta	Zip Code	Phone
Patty	Richards	345 W. Mill Ave.	Mesa	AZ	84101-748	(602) 55
Julie	Wendale	125 N. Marigold St.	Tempe	AZ	86301-128	(602) 55
Scott	Samuals	90 First Ave.	Phoenix	AZ	82891-160	(602) 55
Student	Name	89 Any Street	Mesa	AZ	85202-	(602)55
*				AZ		

Form Datasheet view provides a datasheet view of the form data. Although it appears similar to Table Datasheet view, Form Datasheet view includes all fields from the form, including calculated fields.

Notice that the field columns are in the same order as in the form. Form Datasheet view also reflects the same field order as in the form. The Table Datasheet view, however, has not been affected by the changes you made in the form layout. Also notice that the new records are not in primary key order by employee number. When you open the table in Datasheet view, the new records will appear in primary key order.

You can also click in the vertical bar at the left edge of the Form window to select the record.

Previewing and Printing a Form

You want to preview, then print just the form displaying your record.

■ Switch back to Form view.

■ Check [🔍] Print Preview.

Your screen should be similar to Figure 2-28.

Form name

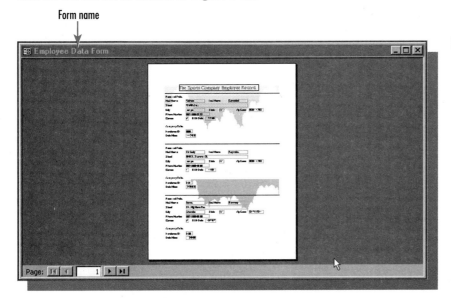

FIGURE 2-28

Form Print Preview displays whatever view of the form you were just looking at in the preview window. In this case, because you were last in Form view, the form is displayed in the preview window. The form header appears at the top of the page and three records appear below the header. You want to print only the form displaying your record. To do this,

- Return to Form view and display your record in the form.

- Choose **Edit/Select Record.**

- Choose **File/Print.**

- Select Selected **R**ecord(s).

- Click [OK].

Closing and Saving a Form

Next you will close and save the form.

- Close the Form window.

- Click [Yes].

The Database window is displayed, showing the new form object name in the Forms tab object list.

- Exit Access.

Do not remove your data disk from the drive until you exit Access.

LAB REVIEW

■ ■ ■ ■ ■ ■ ■ ■ ▪ ▫ ▫

Key Terms

bound control (DB70)
calculated control (DB70)
character string (DB53)
compound control (DB78)
control (DB70)
expression (DB64)
font (DB83)
form (DB70)
identifier (DB64)

input mask (DB54)
label control (DB70)
literal character (DB54)
mask character (DB54)
move handle (DB78)
operator (DB64)
points (DB83)
sizing handles (DB78)
sort (DB67)

tab order (DB72)
text box control (DB70)
typeface (DB83)
unbound control (DB70)
validation text (DB64)
validity check (DB64)
value (DB64)

Command Summary

Command	Shortcut	Toolbar	Action
Edit/**U**ndo	Ctrl + Z	↺	Cancels last action
Edit/**Cu**t	Ctrl + X or Delete	✄ or ✄	Deletes selected record
Edit/Se**l**ect Record	⇧Shift + Spacebar		Selects current record
Edit/Select **A**ll	Ctrl + A		Selects all controls on a form in Form Design view
Edit/**F**ind	Ctrl + F	🔍	Locates specified data
Edit/Re**p**lace	Ctrl + H		Locates and replaces specified data
View/**D**esign View		📐	Display a form in Design view
View/**F**orm View		📋	Display a form in Form view
View/Data**s**heet View		📊	Display a form in Datasheet view
Insert/**F**ield			Inserts a new field in table in Design view
F**o**rmat/**H**ide Columns			Hides columns in Datasheet view
F**o**rmat/**U**nhide Columns			Redisplays hidden columns in Datasheet view
F**o**rmat/A**l**ign/**L**eft			Aligns selected controls to left
F**o**rmat/**S**ize/To **F**it			Automatically resizes a control to fit contents
F**o**rmat/**V**ertical Spacing/Make **E**qual			Equalizes vertical space between selected multiple controls
Records/**S**ort/**A**scending		⇣	Reorders records in ascending alphabetical order

Matching

1. operator	_____	**a.** links a form to the underlying table
2. sizing handles	_____	**b.** used to check that value entered in a field is valid for field type
3. [Aa]	_____	**c.** database object used primarily for onscreen display
4. ="Accounting" or "Finance"	_____	**d.** adds a text label control to form
5. control	_____	**e.** symbol, such as = or AND, that indicates operation to be performed
6. >	_____	**f.** example of an expression that would limit data that could be entered in a field
7. sort	_____	**g.** toolbar button to locate specified data
8. validity check	_____	**h.** small boxes that surround a selected control
9. [icon]	_____	**i.** changes display order of a table
10. form	_____	**j.** format character that forces all data in field to uppercase

Fill-In Questions

1. Complete the following statements by filling in the blanks with the correct terms.

a. A(n) _____ is a combination of symbols that produces specific results.

b. The _____ property is used to specify a value that is automatically entered in a field when a new record is created.

c. When _____ are performed, Access makes sure that the entry is acceptable in the field.

d. Records can be temporarily displayed in a different order by using the _____ feature.

e. Forms are primarily used for _____ and making changes to existing records.

f. The _____ property changes the way data appears in a field.

g. The four form layouts are _____, _____, _____, and _____.

h. A(n) _____ is a pattern that controls the data that can be entered in a field.

i. When a form control in selected, it is surrounded by _____.

j. A(n) _____ is the design and shape of characters.

Discussion Questions

1. Discuss several different format properties and how they are used in a database.

2. Discuss why you would use input masks in a database. Give several examples of input masks and describe how they would affect the entry of data in a field.

3. Describe the three types of controls and give examples of each.

4. Discuss how validity checks work. What are some advantages of adding validity checks to a field? Include several examples.

5. Discuss the different ways records can be sorted. What are some advantages of sorting records?

Hands-On Practice Exercises

■ ■ ■ ■ ■ ■ ■ ■ ▧ ▢

Step by Step   **Rating System**   ☆ Easy
                                                      ☆☆ Moderate
                                                      ☆☆☆ Difficult

1. James O'Dell at Valley of the Sun Office Supplies has created a database to track inventory.

   a. Open the Valley of the Sun Office Supplies database and the Inventory table. Make the following changes to the records indicated:

Item #78564	should read "clips," not "blips"
Item #28765	should indicate 10 Rolls/Box
Item #18719	has 8 pens in stock, not 863
Item #25743	price is $18.50 not $185.00

   b. Using the Find command, find item #53410 and enter the correct item number, 54301.

   c. Add a field property to the Item Name field to force the data in the field to display in all capital letters.

   d. Enter the item number 99999 in the Item # field and your name in the Item Name field of a new record. Resize the Item Name column. Sort the table by Item Name, then print the table.

   e. Return the table to the primary key sort order.

   f. Close the table, saving any changes.

2. Michelle owns Food for Thought Catering. As her catering business continues to grow, she has established a reputation for excellent gourmet health foods. Nevertheless, she continues to serve whatever kinds of food her customers request. She wants your assistance to help her customize her database of client records.

   a. Open the Food for Thought Catering database and the Customers table.

   b. To help Michelle track which customers prefer healthy foods, in Table Design view, add a field after the Preferred Theme field. Use the following guidelines to define the new field:

Field name:	Healthy Foods
Data type:	Text
Description:	Does client prefer health-conscious foods?
Field size:	8
Format:	Display in all capital letters
Validation rule:	"Always" or "Never" or "Optional"
Validation text:	"Selection must be either Always, Never, or Optional"

   c. Update the table by entering an option in the Healthy Foods field for each record.

   d. Using the Form Wizard, create a columnar form. Use the Colorful 2 style. Title the new form "Customer Information Form." In Design view, move the controls to make the computerized form look similar to Michelle's current paper form shown below. Also add the label for the title and a subhead for the Customer Preferences section of the form as shown in the paper form.

Customer Information Form

Customer #:
Company:
Contact: Phone:
Address:
City: State: Zipcode:

Customer Preferences

Healthy Food?
Preferred Theme?
Favorite Dish?

---

   e. In Form Design view, make these enhancements to the form:

   ■ Increase the font size for all controls to 12 points.

- Change the font for the Customer Information Form label control to a typeface of your choice and to 20 points, then size the control to fit.

- Change the font for the Customer Preferences label control to 14-point italic, then size the control to fit and underline the text.

f. Add these new customers to the table using the new form:

Customer Information Form

Customer #: 27691
Company: Desert Rescue Cleaning Service
Contact: Debbie Harrington   Phone: 212-3999
Address: 6730 E. Ray Rd.
City: Chandler
State: AZ
Zipcode: 85601

Customer Preferences

Healthy Food? Always
Preferred Theme? Merry Maids
Favorite Dish? Souffle

Customer Information Form

Customer #: 41476
Company: Sunset Publishing
Contact: Jessica Herrera   Phone: 999-6110
Address: 3276 S. Rural Rd.
City: Tempe
State: AZ
Zipcode: 89562

Customer Preferences

Healthy Food? Always
Preferred Theme? Library
Favorite Dish? Spinach Salad

---

g. Adjust the size of any controls as needed to display the data appropriately. Adjust the alignment and vertical spacing of controls as needed.

h. Display the record for The Sports Company in the form. Change the contact name to your name. Print the record.

3. Eddie Fitzpatrick of TechnoBabble Electronics heard from Michelle at Food for Thought Catering that you are great with Access databases. Eddie needs you to help him customize the database that his cousin Teddy helped him set up. He has been putting in records, but doesn't know how to edit the data or to create a data entry form.

a. Open the TechnoBabble Electronics database and the Inventory table. Make these changes to the records:

Item #7195: change 100 to 133 in the Description field

Item #8031: change sEcurty to Security in the Description field

In all records where MPS is the supplier, change MPS to CTC.

b. Teddy created sample entries for the table while Eddie was learning how to use the database. You now need to delete those records. Delete records for items #5640, #5926, and #6832.

c. Find item #8205 and change the cost from $200 to $150.

d. In Table Design view, add a field for the purchase price between Cost and Quantity on Hand, with these specifications:

Field name:	Purchase Price
Data type:	Currency
Description:	Cost to Customer

e. Add a field between Shelf Location and Supplier for the status of each item, indicating whether it is a regularly stocked item or a special order item. Use these specifications:

Field name:	Status
Data type:	Text
Description:	What is the stocking status of this item?
Field size:	9
Format:	Display in all capital letters
Default value:	STOCK
Validation rule:	Stock or SpecOrder
Validation text:	Stocking status must be either Stock or SpecOrder

f. Change the Quantity on Hand field name to # On Hand, and the Shelf Location field name to Shelf. Change the supplies description to "3-character supplier code."

g. Add customer prices and stocking status to the existing data in the table.

h. Sort the table on the Description field, resize the columns, then print the table.

i. Return the table to the primary key sort order.

j. Create a columnar form for Eddie using the Form Wizard. Use the Evergreen background and name the form TechnoBabble Electronics Inventory List.

k. In Form Design view, move the controls so the form layout looks similar to Eddie's existing data entry form shown below. Add the label controls to display the form title and the Confidential subhead. Adjust the alignment and vertical spacing of controls as reached.

```
TechnoBabble Electronics Inventory List

Item #:_____
Description: _____
Shelf:_____ # On Hand:_____
Purchase Price: _____

Confidential
Supplier:_____
Status:_____ Cost:_____
```

l. In Form Design view, enhance the form by making these changes:

- Change the form title text to yellow.
- Bold all controls in the form.
- Change all controls to 10-point Times New Roman.
- Change the text in the title control to a typeface of your choice and 18 points, then size the control to fit.
- Change the text in the Confidential control to 14-point Arial italic, then size the control to fit.
- Enlarge the Status text box control.

m. Using the form, enter the following two new records:

```
TechnoBabble Electronics Inventory List

Item #: 2317
Description: Pager
Shelf: B-21          # On Hand: 4
Purchase Price: $74.50

Confidential
Supplier: CTC
Status: STOCK          Cost: $32.95
```

```
TechnoBabble Electronics Inventory List

Item #: 9611
Description: Keyboard, Electronic Music
Shelf: H-01          # On Hand: 1
Purchase Price: $324.35

Confidential
Supplier: MEE
Status: SPECORDER     Cost: $178.50
```

n. While looking at the form, you notice several controls are not sized appropriately for the data they display. Return to Design view and adjust the textbox controls as needed.

o. Use the Find command to locate the record for Item #3910. Add your name in the Description field. Select, then print the record. Close the form, saving any changes.

On Your Own

4. Debbie owns Desert Rescue Cleaning Service. Her commercial cleaning business is prospering, and she has asked you to help her by entering some new data and customizing her database of client records.

Open the Desert Rescue Cleaning Service database and the Clients table, then add five new records with either real or fictitious data. Change the contact in The Sports Company record to your name. Adjust the column widths as necessary.

Make any changes to the field properties that would make data entry easier, such as adding format properties or validation rules.

Use the Form Wizard to create a columnar form for data entry, named Desert Rescue Cleaning Service Client Data Form, arranging the controls to make data entry easy. Remember to add a title and any other helpful information on the form as a label.

Find the record for The Sports Company and print that form.

5. Michael has just contacted you from Go West Dude Ranch. The database you helped Michael create is working well, but he needs to make some changes. He is adding clients daily. Most of the clients are medium-sized companies who rent the Dude Ranch for special company functions, meetings, or other corporate events. Michael would like to track these customers. Help him with the database by making the following changes:

Open the Go West Dude Ranch database. Add a phone number field and data to the Staff table. Create a new table named Business Clients to track clients. Include an identification field and a contact person for each company. Remember to create a primary key field. Use appropriate field properties to make data entry easier.

Add three new business clients to the table. Adjust the display so that all information is displayed in each column. Sort the data by company name, then print the table. Return the order to primary key order. Remember to save any layout changes to the table.

Create a columnar form based on the Business Clients table for entering new clients into the table, and name it Go West Dude Ranch New Client Information. Enter three more new clients, including The Sports Company, making yourself the contact person for the company. Print that record form.

Create a columnar form named Go West Dude Ranch Employees, based on the Staff Records table, for the employees table that you helped Michael create earlier. You have agreed to take on another part-time job helping Michael out at the Dude Ranch in the Data Processing department, so enter a record for yourself using the new form, then print your record.

6. You are looking for a new job. To keep track of all the companies you have contacted, you decide to create a database file of this information.

Name the database file My Contacts. Create a table named Contacts that includes fields such as the company name, address, phone number, name of the contact person, and type of company. Include a field that is a unique number that you can assign each record. Make this field the primary key. Include other fields that you can use to track your status with the company, for example, fields that indicate the date a resume was sent, a phone contact was made, or the date of an interview.

Add appropriate field properties, such as formats, validation rules, and input masks. Enter at least five records. Print the table.

Create a columnar form named [Your Name] Employment Contacts. Use the form to add five additional records. Print one record.

Modifying a Table and Creating a Form

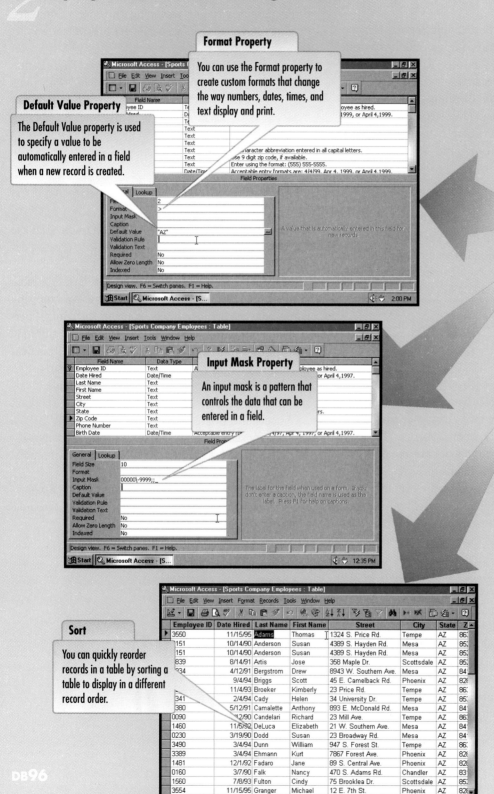

Format Property

You can use the Format property to create custom formats that change the way numbers, dates, times, and text display and print.

Default Value Property

The Default Value property is used to specify a value to be automatically entered in a field when a new record is created.

Input Mask Property

An input mask is a pattern that controls the data that can be entered in a field.

Sort

You can quickly reorder records in a table by sorting a table to display in a different record order.

Concepts

Format Property
Default Value Property

Input Mask Property

Find and Replace

Validity Checks

Sort

Forms
Fonts

Find and Replace

The ability to quickly find specific information and automatically replace it with new information is one of the main advantages of a computerized database.

Validity Checks

Access automatically performs certain checks, called validity checks, on values entered in a field to make sure that the values are valid for the field type.

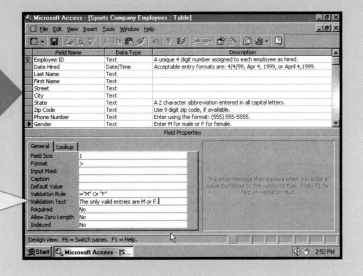

Fonts

Fonts consist of three elements: typeface, size, and style that can be applied to characters to improve their appearance.

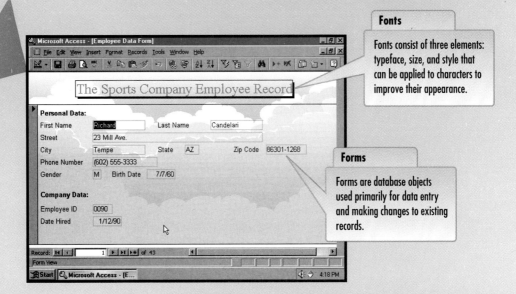

Forms

Forms are database objects used primarily for data entry and making changes to existing records.

Filtering and Querying Tables

CASE STUDY

You are satisfied with the structure of the table of employee records and have entered many more records. You have also created several other tables that contain employee data such as pay rates and job titles. However, compiling, storing, and updating information in your database is useful only if you can find the information you need quickly, and can manipulate it and analyze it to answer specific questions.

You will use the information in the tables to provide the answers to several inquiries about The Sports Company employees. As you learn about the analytical features, think what it would be like to do the same task by hand. How long would it take? Would it be as accurate or as well presented? Your appreciation grows as you learn more about what the application can do for you. The output from one of your inquiries is shown here.

Department	Last Name	First Name	Hourly Rate	New Rate
Clothing	Fisher	Sarah	$5.00	$5.38
Sports Equipment	Lawson	Tamara	$5.00	$5.38
Sports Equipment	Moran	Jeannie	$5.00	$5.38
Sports Equipment	Lye	Hin	$5.00	$5.38
Warehouse	Castillo	Blas	$4.50	$4.84
Warehouse	Lockwood	Craig	$5.25	$5.64
Warehouse	Hayes	Carol	$5.00	$5.38
Warehouse	Granger	Michael	$4.50	$4.84
Warehouse	Jessup	Hart	$5.00	$5.38
Warehouse	Fulton	Cindy	$5.00	$5.38

In addition, you will create another form (shown on the right) to be used to update information in several tables simultaneously.

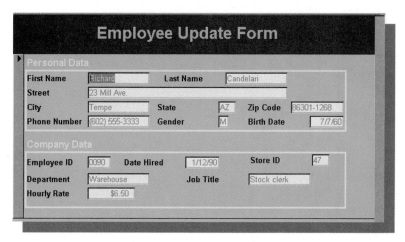

Concept Overview

The following concepts will be introduced in this lab:

1. Filter
A filter is a restriction you place on records in the open datasheet or form to temporarily isolate and display a subset of records.

2. AND and OR Operators
The AND and OR operators are used to specify multiple conditions that must be met for the records to display in the datasheet.

3. Wildcard Characters
Wildcard characters are placeholders that represent any series of characters or any single character.

4. Query
A query is a question you ask of a database that allows you to view data in different ways, to analyze data, and even to change existing data.

5. Joins and Relationships
You can bring information from different tables in your database together by defining a relationship to join the tables.

6. Calculated Field
A calculated field displays the result of a calculation in a query.

Part 1

Using Filter by Selection

You have continued to enter employee records into the Employees table. The updated table has been saved for you as Sports Company Employees in the Sports Company Personnel Records database on your data disk.

■ Start Access 97. Put your data disk in the appropriate drive for your system.

■ Open the Sports Company Personnel Records database file.

The Tables list box of the Database window displays the names of four tables in this database: Sports Company Employees, Weekly Hours Worked, Employee Pay Rates, and Employees by Department and Position. These tables will be used throughout the lab.

■ Open the Sports Company Employees table.

■ If necessary, maximize the table Datasheet window.

■ Add your information as record number 73 using your special ID number 9999 and the current date as your hire date.

While you are using the table, the manager asks you for two items of information. The first is a request from an employee who wants to form a carpool. The employee wants to know the names of other employees who live in her town. The second is to help figure out the name of the employee who recently sent the manager a memo. The memo suggested how the warehouse could save time and money by changing one of the reporting procedures it uses. Although the first

DATABASE

name in the memo is legible, the last name is not. The manager can only make out the first letter of the last name, C.

To answer both questions, you could sort the table and then write down the needed information. However, this could be time consuming if you had hundreds of employees in the table. A faster way is to apply a filter to the table records to locate this information.

> **Concept 1: Filter**
>
> A **filter** is a restriction you place on records in the open datasheet or form to quickly isolate and display a subset of records. A filter is created by specifying a set of limiting conditions, or **criteria**, you want records to meet in order to be displayed. A filter is ideal when you only want to display the subset for a brief time, then return immediately to the full set of records. You can print the filtered records as you would any form or table. A filter is only temporary and all records are redisplayed when you remove the filter or close and reopen the table or form. The filter results cannot be saved. However, the last filter criteria you specify are saved with the table and the results can be quickly redisplayed.

To find only those employees in the city of Chandler, you can quickly filter out all the other records using the Filter by Selection method. **Filter by Selection** is used when you can easily find and select an instance of the value in the table that you want the filter to use as the criterion to meet.

How the value is selected determines what results will be displayed. Placing the insertion point in a field selects the entire field contents. The filtered subset will include all records containing an exact match. Selecting part of a value in a field (by highlighting it) displays all records containing the selection. For example, in a table for a book collection, you could position the mouse pointer anywhere in a field containing the name of the author Stephen King, choose the Filter by Selection command, and only records for books whose author matches the selected name, "Stephen King," would be displayed. Selecting the last name "King" would include all records for authors Stephen King, Martin Luther King, and Barbara Kingsolver.

You want to filter the table to display only those records with a City field entry of Chandler. To specify the city to locate, you need to select an example of the data in the table.

- Move to the City field of record 3.

- Click ▒ Filter by Selection.

If the selected part of a value starts with the first character in the field, the subset displays all records whose values begin with the same selected characters.

The menu equivalent is **R**ecords/**F**ilter/Filter by **S**election.

Your screen should be similar to Figure 3-1.

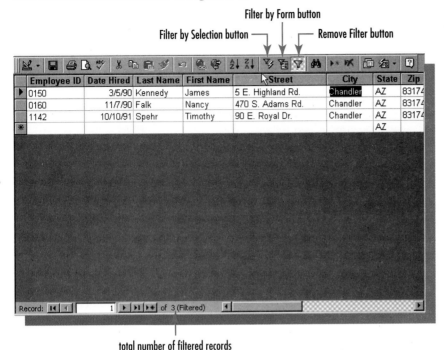

FIGURE 3-1

The datasheet displays only those records that contain the selected city. All other records are temporarily hidden. The status bar indicates the total number of filtered records and shows that the datasheet is filtered. To remove the filter,

■ Click 🔽 Remove Filter.

Using Filter by Form

After seeing how easy it was to locate this information, the manager asks you to also locate employees who live in the city of Mesa. This information may help in setting up the carpool, since the people traveling from the city of Chandler pass through Mesa on the way to the store. To find out this additional information, you need to use the **Filter by Form** method. This method allows you to perform filters on multiple criteria.

■ Click 📋 Filter by Form.

You can print the filtered datasheet like any other datasheet.

The menu equivalent is **Records/Remove Filter/Sort**.

The menu equivalent is **Records/Filter/Filter By Form**.

Your screen should be similar to Figure 3-2.

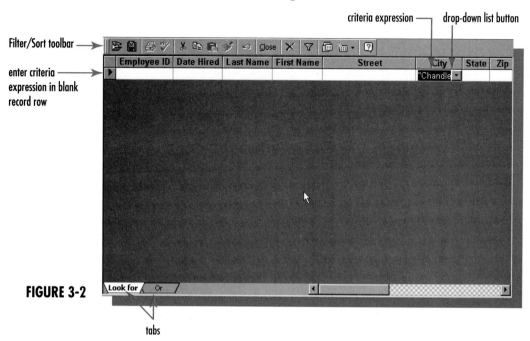

FIGURE 3-2

tabs

The Filter by Form window displays a blank version of the current datasheet with empty fields in which you specify the criteria. This window automatically displays a Filter/Sort toolbar that contains the standard buttons as well as buttons (identified below) that are specific to the Filter by Form window.

> Refer to Concept 6: Validity Checks in Lab 2 to review expressions.

The window also includes two tabs, Look For and Or, where you enter the filter criteria. The criteria are entered in the blank field space of the record row as an expression. A **criteria expression** specifies the criteria for the filter to use. You can either type values or choose values from a drop-down list in the desired field to create the criteria expression.

Currently the City field displays the criterion you last specified using Filter by Selection as the criteria expression. Notice that the field displays a drop-down list button. Each field will display a drop-down button when the field is selected. Clicking the button displays a list of values that are available in that field from which you can select to help you enter the criteria expression.

Since the City field already contains the correct criterion, you do not need to enter a different criterion. Next, you need to add the second criterion to the filter to include all records with a City field value of Mesa. To instruct the filter to locate records meeting multiple criteria, you use the AND or OR operators.

Concept 2: AND and OR Operators

The AND and OR operators are used to specify multiple conditions that must be met for the records to display in the filter datasheet. The AND operator narrows the search, because a record must meet both conditions to be included. The OR operator broadens the search, because any record meeting either condition is included in the output.

The AND operator is assumed when you enter criteria in multiple fields. Within a field, typing the word "AND" between criteria in the same field establishes the AND condition. For example, in the book table you could enter "Stephen King" in the author name field, then you could enter "Horror" in the category field to display records where the author's name is Stephen King and the category is Horror.

The OR operator is established by entering the criterion in the Or tab, or by typing "OR" between criteria in the same field. For example, you could enter "Stephen King" in the author name field, select the Or tab, then enter "Horror" in the category field. This filter would display those records where the author's name is Stephen King or where the category is Horror.

In this filter you will use an OR operator so that records meeting either city criterion will be included in the output. To include the city as an OR criterion, you enter the criterion in the Or tab.

■ Click **Or**.

The Or tab is opened and a new blank row is displayed. You will enter the expression specifying the criterion by selecting the criterion from the City drop-down list.

■ Click ▼ (in the City field).

■ Choose Mesa.

A value must be entered in the Look For tab before the Or tab is available.

You could also have entered the expression "Chandler" or "Mesa" in the City field of the Look For tab.

Chandler
Mesa
Phoenix
Scottsdale
Tempe

DATABASE

Your screen should be similar to Figure 3-3.

FIGURE 3-3

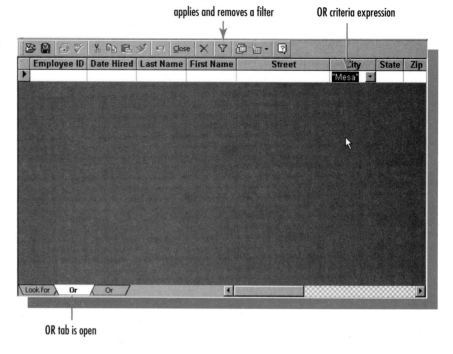

The selected criterion is displayed in the City field. It is surrounded by quotes, as required of all text entries used in an expression. The Look For tab still contains the criteria for city of Chandler. To apply the filter,

■ Click ▽ Apply filter.

The filtered datasheet displays the records for all 21 employees who live in the city of Chandler or Mesa.

Your screen should be similar to Figure 3-4.

▽ is a toggle button that applies and removes a filter.

The menu equivalent is Filter/Apply Filter/Sort.

FIGURE 3-4

Employee ID	Date Hired	Last Name	First Name	Street	City	State	Z
0150	3/5/90	Kennedy	James	5 E. Highland Rd.	Chandler	AZ	83
0151	10/14/90	Anderson	Susan	4389 S. Hayden Rd.	Mesa	AZ	85
0160	11/7/90	Falk	Nancy	470 S. Adams Rd.	Chandler	AZ	83
0230	12/19/90	Dodd	Susan	23 Broadway Rd.	Mesa	AZ	84
0234	4/12/91	Bergstrom	Drew	8943 W. Southern Ave.	Mesa	AZ	84
0380	5/12/91	Camalette	Anthony	893 E. McDonald Rd.	Mesa	AZ	84
1142	10/10/91	Spehr	Timothy	90 E. Royal Dr.	Chandler	AZ	83
1241	1/7/92	Williamson	Anthony	89 College Ave.	Mesa	AZ	84
1460	11/5/92	DeLuca	Elizabeth	21 W. Southern Ave.	Mesa	AZ	84
2300	8/16/93	Richards	Carman	5401 E. Thomas Rd.	Mesa	AZ	84
2320	12/1/93	Jessup	Hart	432 E. Rider Rd.	Mesa	AZ	84
2322	12/1/93	Smith	Bonnie	564 S. Lemon Dr.	Mesa	AZ	84
3500	9/4/94	Henkenius	Glenda	923 E. Baseline Rd.	Mesa	AZ	84
3561	11/21/95	Richards	Patty	345 W. Mill Ave.	Mesa	AZ	84
4158	4/4/96	Steele	Cynthia	2515 E. Elmwood Dr.	Mesa	AZ	84
4189	8/15/96	McLean	Karen	4601 E. Willow Dr.	Mesa	AZ	84
4191	8/15/96	Hayes	Carol	7115 E. Roosevelt Dr.	Mesa	AZ	84
4200	9/9/96	Lye	Hin	889 S. Litchfield Park	Mesa	AZ	84

Record: 1 of 21 (Filtered)

A unique 4 digit number assigned to each employee as hired.   FLTR

The manager's second request is to locate the employee whose last name begins with the letter C. This filter requires that you enter an expression in the Last Name field. To clear all existing expressions from the Filter Form window,

- ■ Click ⌦ Filter by Form.

- ■ Click ✕ Clear Grid.

- ■ Move to the Last Name field.

> You do not need to remove a filter before applying another.

> The menu equivalent is **Edit/Clear Grid**.

To specify the criteria to find this employee, you will use a wildcard character in the expression.

Concept 3: Wildcard Characters

Wildcard characters are placeholders in an expression that represent any series of characters or any single character. They specify a value you want to find when you either know only part of the value or want to find all values that begin with a certain letter or match a specific pattern.

The six wildcard characters are described below.

Character	Use	Example
*	Matches any number of characters.	"Smit*" locates Smitt, Smith, Smithers. "*ing" locates all occurrences of values ending in "ing."
?	Matches any single character.	"Smit?" locates Smitt and Smith, but not Smithers. "b?t" locates bet, bit, but, or Bat, but not beat.
[]	Matches any single character within the brackets.	"b[iu]t" locates bit and but, but not bet or bat.
!	Matches any character not in the brackets.	"b[!iu]t" locates bet and bat, but not bit or but.
-	Matches any one of a range of characters that you specify.	"[a-h]eat" locates beat, feat, and heat, but not meat, neat, or seat.
#	Matches any single numeric character.	"1#3" locates 153 or 163, but not 1453 or 19653.

The expression C* will find any series of characters that follows the letter C.

- ■ Type c*

- ■ Press ⎮←Enter⎮.

> The letter can be entered in either upper- or lowercase, because Access is not case sensitive.

Access automatically converts the entry you typed to "Like 'c*'." Access gives you flexibility in the way you enter expressions, but it will convert what you type into expressions displaying the correct rules or syntax for the expression. In this case Access added the LIKE operator to the expression and enclosed the expression in double quotation marks. If you do not include an operator when using wildcard characters, Access automatically enters the appropriate operator for you.

criteria expression with
wildcard character

Last Name
Like "c*"

■ Click 🔽 Apply Filter.

Your screen should be similar to Figure 3-5.

FIGURE 3-5

Employee ID	Date Hired	Last Name	First Name	Street	City	State	Zip
▶ 0090	1/12/90	Candelari	Richard	23 Mill Ave.	Tempe	AZ	86301
0380	5/12/91	Camalette	Anthony	893 E. McDonald Rd.	Mesa	AZ	84101
2341	2/4/94	Cady	Helen	34 University Dr.	Tempe	AZ	85301
4255	3/2/97	Carrier	Kirk	932 E. Parkway Dr.	Mesa	AZ	84101
4269	5/3/97	Castillo	Blas	382 E. Meadow Ave.	Phoenix	AZ	82891
*						AZ	

The filtered datasheet displays the records for all employees (five) whose last names begin with the letter C. Now the manager can determine which employee sent the memo.

To redisplay all records in the table and continue working.

■ Click 🔽 Remove Filter.

■ Close the Sports Company Employees table (save your changes).

The filter criteria you last specified are saved with the table, and the results can be redisplayed simply by applying the filter.

Creating a Query

Your next request for information is for a list of all employees and their hire dates. Although you could use a filter to get the information, a filter displays the entire record. You want the list to display only the employees' names and hire dates. To create this list, you need to use a query.

Concept 4: Query

A **query** is a question you ask of the data contained in your database. You use queries to view data in different ways, to analyze data, and even to change existing data. Since queries are based on tables, you can also use a query as the source for forms and reports. The five types of queries are described in the table below.

Query Type	Description
Select query	Retrieves the specific data you request from one or more tables, then displays the data in a query datasheet in the order you specify. This is the most common type of query.
Crosstab query	Summarizes large amounts of data in an easy-to-read, row-and-column format.
Parameter query	Displays a dialog box prompting you for information, such as criteria for locating data. For example, a parameter query might request the beginning and ending dates, then display all records matching dates between the two specified values.
Action query	Makes changes to many records in one operation. There are four types of action queries: a make-table query creates a new table from selected data in one or more tables; an update query makes update changes to records, such as when you need to raise salaries of all sales staff by 7 percent; an append query adds records from one or more tables to the end of other tables; and a delete query deletes records from a table or tables.
SQL query	Created using SQL (Structured Query Language), an advanced programming language used in Access.

To create a new query,

- Open the Queries tab.

- Click [New].

The New Query dialog box contains five options for creating queries. You can create a query from scratch in Query Design view or by using one of the four Query Wizards. The table on the next page explains the type of query each of the four wizards creates.

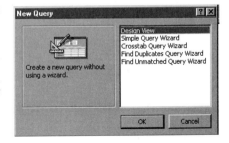

Query Wizard	Type of Query Created
Simple	Select query
Crosstab	Crosstab query
Find Duplicates	Locates all records that contain duplicate values in one or more fields in the specified tables
Find Unmatched	Locates records in one table that do not have records in another. For example, you could locate all employees in one table who have no hours worked in another table.

To create a select query using the Simple Query Wizard,

- Select Simple Query Wizard.

- Click [OK].

In the first Simple Query Wizard window (shown in Figure 3-6), you specify the table and the fields from the table that will give you the desired query result. You need a list of employees and hire dates from the Sports Company Employees table.

- Open the Table/Queries drop-down list.

- Select Table: Sports Company Employees.

- Add the Date Hired, Last Name and First Name fields to the Selected Fields list.

> Double-click the field name in the Available Fields list to add it to the Selected Fields list.

The dialog box on your screen should be similar to Figure 3-6.

FIGURE 3-6

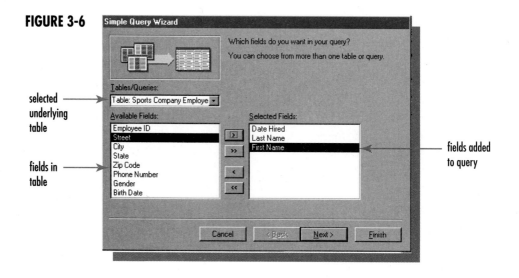

■ Click [Next >].

■ Replace the suggested title in the text box with "Hire Date."

■ Click [Finish].

After a few moments, your screen should be similar to Figure 3-7.

Query Datasheet view displays query results

Date Hired	Last Name	First Name
1/12/90	Candelari	Richard
2/20/90	Reynolds	Kimberly
3/5/90	Kennedy	James
10/14/90	Anderson	Susan
11/7/90	Falk	Nancy
12/19/90	Dodd	Susan
4/12/91	Bergstrom	Drew
4/21/91	Steverson	Toni
5/12/91	Camalette	Anthony
6/4/91	Long	William
6/10/91	Reynolds	Cara
6/15/91	Hanson	Kevin
7/15/91	Toroyan	Lucy
8/14/91	Artis	Jose
9/12/91	Smith	Brent
10/10/91	Spehr	Timothy
1/7/92	Williamson	Anthony
2/1/92	Little	Jennifer

Record: |◄| ◄ | 1 | ► | ►| | ►* | of 73

FIGURE 3-7

The result or answer to the query is displayed in a **query datasheet**. The query datasheet displays only the three specified fields for all records in the table. Query Datasheet view includes the same menus and toolbar buttons as in Table Datasheet view.

Moving Columns

The order of the fields in the query datasheet reflects the order they were placed in the Selected Fields list. However, the manager wants the list of names to be organized with the first name before the last name. You can change the display order of the fields by moving the columns. To reorder columns, first select the column you want to move and then drag the selection to its new location. You want to move the First Name column to the left of the Last Name column.

■ Select the First Name column.

■ Click and hold the mouse button on the First Name column heading.

■ Drag the First Name column to the left until a thick black line is displayed between the Date Hired and Last Name columns. Release the mouse button.

■ Clear the selection.

Reminder: Click on the First Name column heading when the mouse pointer is a ↓ to select it.

When the mouse pointer is a ↖, it indicates you can drag to move the selection.

The keyboard equivalent is [Ctrl] + [F8] to turn on Move mode. Then press [←] or [→] to move the column in the desired direction, then press [Esc].

Your screen should be similar to Figure 3-8.

First Name column moved to new location

FIGURE 3-8

Date Hired	First Name	Last Name
1/12/90	Richard	Candelari
2/20/90	Kimberly	Reynolds
3/5/90	James	Kennedy
10/14/90	Susan	Anderson
11/7/90	Nancy	Falk
12/19/90	Susan	Dodd
4/12/91	Drew	Bergstrom
4/21/91	Toni	Steverson
5/12/91	Anthony	Camalette
6/4/91	William	Long

> You can move fields in Table Datasheet view in the same manner.

Now the query datasheet is displayed in the order requested by the manager. Changing the column order in the query datasheet does not affect the field order in the table, which is controlled by the table design.

Querying Using Comparison Operators

The manager would like to recognize the employees who have worked with The Sports Company for at least five years. To help the manager locate these employees, you can modify the Hire Date query to create a list of all employees who were hired before January of 1992.

The query datasheet is based on settings that were entered in the Query Design window by the Wizard. To see the Query Design view,

■ Click 📐 Design View.

Your screen should be similar to Figure 3-9.

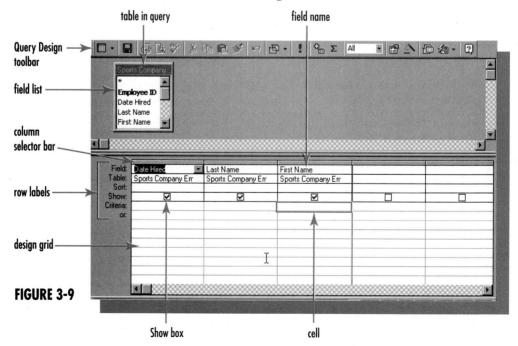

table in query

field name

Query Design toolbar

field list

column selector bar

row labels

design grid

FIGURE 3-9

Show box

cell

The Query Design view is used to create and modify the structure of the query. This view automatically displays a Query Design toolbar that contains the standard buttons as well as buttons (identified below) that are specific to the Query Design view window.

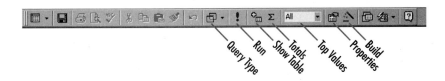

The Query Design window is divided into two areas. The upper area displays a list box of all the fields in the selected table. This is called the **field list**. The lower portion of the window displays the **design grid**, where the settings that are used to define the query are displayed. Each column in the grid holds the information about each field to be included in the query datasheet. The design grid currently displays the Date Hired, Last Name, and First Name fields. Above the field names is a narrow bar called the **column selector bar**. It is used to select an entire column. Each row label identifies the type of information that can be entered. The intersection of a column and row creates a **cell**. This is where you enter expressions to obtain the query results you need. Notice the boxes, called Show boxes, in the Show row. The Show box is checked for each field. This indicates that the query result will display the field column.

In the Criteria row of the Date Hired column, you need to enter a criteria expression to locate only those records where the date hired is prior to January 1992. To specify the criterion, you will enter an expression that contains a comparison operator. A **comparison operator** is used to compare two values. The comparison operators are = (equal to) <> (not equal to), < (less than), > (greater than), <= (less than or equal to), and >= (greater than or equal to). You will use the < comparison operator to locate all records with a date less than 1/1/92. To specify the criterion,

■ Move to the Date Hired Criteria cell.

■ Type <1/1/92

■ Press ⏎Enter.

Your screen should be similar to Figure 3-10.

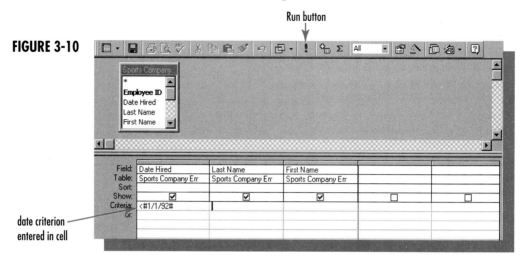

Run button

FIGURE 3-10

date criterion
entered in cell

The expression appears in the cell as <#1/1/92#. Access adds # signs around the date to identify the values in the expression as a date.

To display the query results, you run the query.

■ Click **!** Run.

Your screen should be similar to Figure 3-11.

FIGURE 3-11

Date Hired	Last Name	First Name
1/12/90	Candelari	Richard
2/20/90	Reynolds	Kimberly
3/5/90	Kennedy	James
10/14/90	Anderson	Susan
11/7/90	Falk	Nancy
12/19/90	Dodd	Susan
4/12/91	Bergstrom	Drew
4/21/91	Steverson	Toni
5/12/91	Camalette	Anthony
6/4/91	Long	William
6/10/91	Reynolds	Cara
6/15/91	Hanson	Kevin
7/15/91	Toroyan	Lucy
8/14/91	Artis	Jose
9/12/91	Smith	Brent
10/10/91	Spehr	Timothy

query result shows
records whose date
hired is prior to 1/1/92

Record: 14 ◀ 1 ▶ ▶l ▶* of 16

The menu equivalent is **Q**uery/**R**un. You can also click 🔲 Datasheet View to run the query and display the query datasheet.

Click 🖨, or use **F**ile/**P**rint if you need to specify printer settings.

The query datasheet displays only those records meeting the date criterion. The record number indicator of the query datasheet shows that 16 employees were hired before January 1992. Notice that the fields are again in the order in which they appear in the Design grid.

■ Move the First Name column before the Last Name column.

■ Print a copy of the query datasheet for the manager.

Specifying Multiple Criteria in a Query

Because many of the requests you get for information ask you to locate records using more than one criterion, you decide to practice creating queries using multiple criteria. As in a filter, the AND and OR operators are used to specify several criteria in a query.

First you will query the table to find all employees who have a date hired <1/1/92 *and* have a first name that starts with S. When you enter criteria in separate fields on the same row of the grid, an AND operation is established.

- ■ Switch to the Query Design view.

- ■ Enter **s*** in the First Name Criteria cell.

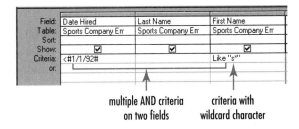

multiple AND criteria   criteria with
on two fields   wildcard character

- ■ Run the query.

The query datasheet shows that two employees were hired before January 1992 and have a first name that starts with S.

Date Hired	First Name	Last Name
▶ 10/14/90	Susan	Anderson
12/19/90	Susan	Dodd
*		

Next you want to see how many employees have a hire date prior to 1/1/92 *or* have a first name that starts with S. When you enter criteria in separate fields on separate rows, an OR operation is established.

- ■ Switch to the Query Design view.

- ■ Remove the criterion from the Criteria cell of the First Name column.

- ■ Enter **s*** in the Or cell of the First Name column.

Field:	Date Hired	Last Name	First Name
Table:	Sports Company Err	Sports Company Err	Sports Company Err
Sort:			
Show:	☑	☑	☑
Criteria:	<#1/1/92#		
or:			Like "s*"

OR criteria on two fields

- ■ Run the query.

To clear cell contents, highlight the entry and press ⎡Delete⎤.

You can use Cut and Paste to move the criterion.

Your screen should be similar to Figure 3-12.

FIGURE 3-12

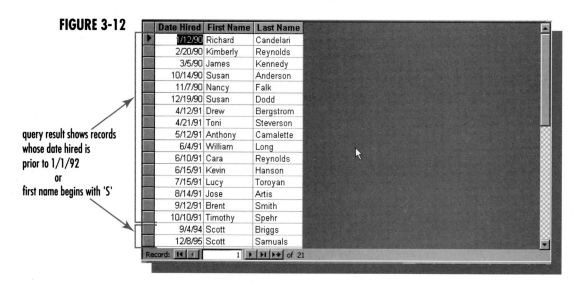

query result shows records
whose date hired is
prior to 1/1/92
or
first name begins with 'S'

The query datasheet displays all records that meet either criterion.

You can also specify multiple criteria in a single field by using the AND and OR operators. The AND condition is established by typing the AND operator in the cell as part of the expression. An OR condition in a single field is established by entering the second criterion in the Or row cell of the same field. To see how this works, you will find out how many employees have a hire date between 1/1/92 and 12/31/93.

■   Switch to Query Design view.

■   Clear the criteria from the Criteria cell in the Date Hired column and from the Or cell in the First Name column.

■   Enter **>=1/1/92 and <=12/31/93** in the Criteria cell of the Date Hired column.

multiple AND criteria on a single field

■   Widen the Date Hired column to fully display the criteria.

■   Run the query.

> Drag the column line to adjust the column width.

> You can also specify the OR operator in a single field in the same manner.

> If an expression is entered incorrectly, an information box is displayed indicating the source of the error.

Your screen should be similar to Figure 3-13.

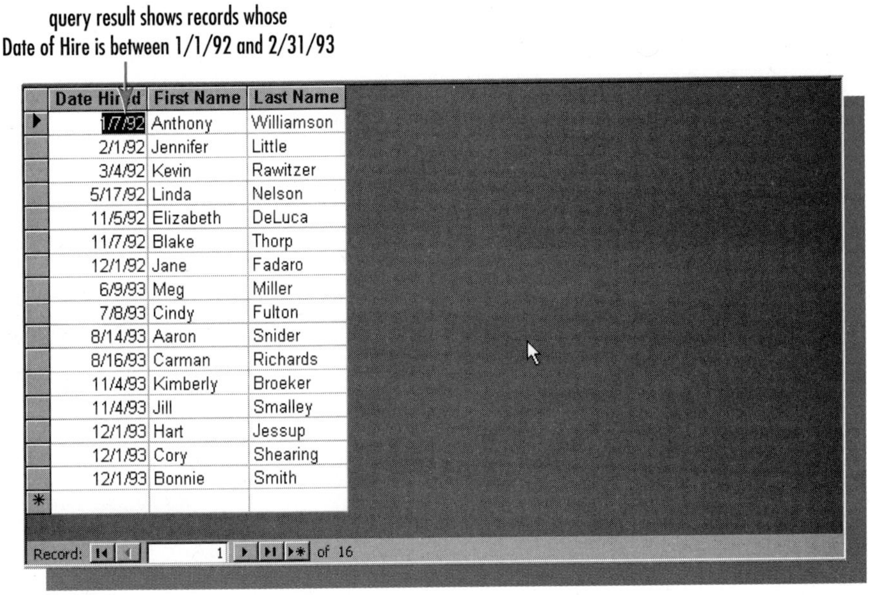

query result shows records whose
Date of Hire is between 1/1/92 and 2/31/93

FIGURE 3-13

Date Hired	First Name	Last Name
1/7/92	Anthony	Williamson
2/1/92	Jennifer	Little
3/4/92	Kevin	Rawitzer
5/17/92	Linda	Nelson
11/5/92	Elizabeth	DeLuca
11/7/92	Blake	Thorp
12/1/92	Jane	Fadaro
6/9/93	Meg	Miller
7/8/93	Cindy	Fulton
8/14/93	Aaron	Snider
8/16/93	Carman	Richards
11/4/93	Kimberly	Broeker
11/4/93	Jill	Smalley
12/1/93	Hart	Jessup
12/1/93	Cory	Shearing
12/1/93	Bonnie	Smith

Record: |◄| |◄| 1 |►| |►►| |►*| of 16

Sixteen records were located in which the hire date met the specified criteria.

■ Close the Query Datasheet window.

■ Save the changes to the query.

The Database window is displayed, and the query name is displayed in the Queries object list.

Note: If you are ending your session now, exit Access. When you begin Part 2, open the Sports Company Personnel Records database file.

Part 2

Querying Two Tables

The manager looked at the list of employees hired before January 1992 and suggested that the query would be more helpful if it included the employee's department. Unfortunately the Sports Company Employees table does not contain this information. This information, however, is available in another table named Employees by Department and Position.

■ From the Tables tab, open the Employees by Department and Position table.

Your screen should be similar to Figure 3-14.

Database Window button

FIGURE 3-14

Employee ID	Store ID	Department	Job Title
0090	47	Warehouse	Stock clerk
0101	68	Sports Equipment	Sales associate
0150	47	Warehouse	Stock clerk
0151	52	Clothing	Sales associate
0160	68	Warehouse	Stock clerk
0230	47	Clothing	Supervisor
0234	52	Operations	Supervisor
0367	47	Operations	Cashier
0380	47	Warehouse	Shipping clerk
0434	47	Sports Equipment	Sales associate
0600	47	Sports Equipment	Sales associate
0650	68	Operations	Cashier
0728	68	Warehouse	Shipping clerk
0839	57	Sports Equipment	Sales associate
1027	68	Operations	Cashier
1142	47	Operations	Head cashier
1241	57	Sports Equipment	Sales associate
1260	57	Sports Equipment	Sales associate

Record: 1 of 73

The Employees by Department and Position table contains four fields of data: Employee ID, Store ID, Department, and Job Title. To display the information the manager wants, you need to create a query using information from this table and from the Sports Company Employee table. A query that uses more than one table is called a **multitable query**.

To switch back to the Database window and create the query from scratch,

> The menu equivalent is **W**indow/**1** Sports Company Personnel Records: Database.

> You can also click on any visible part of the Database window or press F11 to switch to it.

- ■ Click 🔲 Database Window.

- ■ Open the Queries tab.

- ■ Choose ⬛ New ⬛/Design View/ ⬛ OK ⬛.

The Query Design window is open with the Show Table dialog box open on top of it. The dialog box is used to add tables to the query design. The three tabs—Tables, Queries, and Both—contain the names of the existing tables and queries that can be used as the information source for the query. You need to add the Sports Company Employees and the Employees by Department and Position tables to the query design.

- ■ If necessary, open the Tables tab.

- ■ Select Sports Company Employees.

■ Click [Add].

■ Select Employees by Department and Position.

■ Click [Add].

Your screen should be similar to Figure 3-15.

You can also double-click the table name to add it to the query design.

two field lists for selected tables
added to Query Design window

FIGURE 3-15

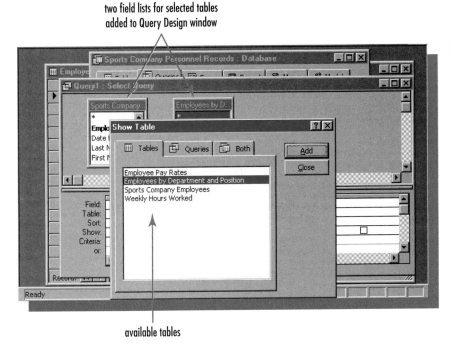

available tables

Field lists for the two selected tables are added to the Query Design window.

■ Close the Show Table dialog box.

■ If necessary, maximize the Query Design window.

The line between the two field lists indicates that the two tables have been temporarily joined.

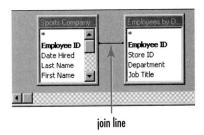

join line

Concept 5: Joins and Relationships

You can bring information from different tables in your database together if you join the tables. A **join** is an association that tells Access how data between tables is related. A **relationship** is established between tables usually through at least one common field. The common fields must be of the same data type and contain the same kind of information, but can have different field names. When you add multiple tables to a query, Access automatically joins tables based on the common fields if one of the common fields is a primary key. This is called the default join or **inner join**. If the common fields have different names, Access does not automatically insert the line and create the join. You can create the join manually by dragging from one common field to the other. The default join instructs the query to check for matching values in the joined fields. When matches are found, the matching data is added to the query datasheet as a single record.

The three types of relationships, one-to-many, many-to-many, and one-to-one, are described in the table below. The most common type is a one-to-many relationship.

Relationship Type	Description
One-to-many	A record in table A can have many matching records in table B, but a record in table B, has only one matching record in table A.
Many-to-many	A record in table A can have many matching records in table B, and a record in table B can have many matching records in table A. This requires a third table in the relationship, known as a junction table, that serves as a bridge between the two tables.
One-to-one	A record in table A has only one matching record in table B, and a record in table B has only one matching record in table A.

More information and examples of relationships are available through the Office Assistant.

Use Tools/Relationships to define permanent relationships between tables.

In a one-to-many relationship there is a primary table and a related or foreign table. The primary table is usually the "one" side of two related tables in a one-to-many relationship, and the related table is usually on the "many" side of a one-to-many relationship.

Using **T**ools/**R**elationships, you can also define permanent relationships between tables that will enforce the rules of **referential integrity**. These rules help ensure that the database always contains accurate and complete data. When these rules are enforced, you cannot add records to a related table when there is no associated record in the primary table. You also cannot change values in the primary table that would result in records that do not have a match in a related table, or delete records from the primary table when there are matching related records in a related table.

The diagram below shows that when the Employee ID fields of the two tables are joined, a query can be created using data from both tables to provide the requested information.

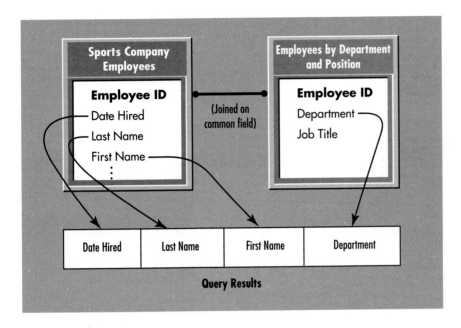

The type of relationship created using these two tables is a one-to-one relationship. This is because each record in the first table has one matching record in the second table.

Next you need to add the fields to the grid that you want to use in the query. The methods you can use to add fields to the design grid are described below.

- Drag the field name from the field list to the grid. You can add several fields at once by pressing ⇧Shift and clicking to select adjacent fields, or by pressing Ctrl and clicking to select nonadjacent fields. When you drag multiple fields at a time, Access places each field in a separate column.

- Double-click on the field name. The field is added to the next available column in the grid.

- Select the Field cell drop-down arrow in the grid, then choose the field name.

> To select all fields, double-click the field list title bar.

In addition, if you select the asterisk in the field list and add it to the grid, Access displays the table or query name in the field row followed by a period and asterisk. All fields in the table are included in the query results. Using this feature also will automatically include any new fields that may later be added to the table and exclude deleted fields. However, you cannot sort records or specify criteria for fields unless you also add those fields individually to the design grid.

includes all fields in table

■ Add the Date Hired, Last Name, First Name, and Department fields, in that order, to the design grid.

■ To specify the date hired criterion, enter the expression **<1/1/92** in the Date Hired Criteria cell.

■ Run the query.

Field:	Date Hired	Last Name	First Name	Department
Table:	Sports Company Err	Sports Company Err	Sports Company Err	Employees by Depa
Sort:				
Show:	☑	☑	☑	☑
Criteria:	<#1/1/92#			
or:				

Your screen should be similar to Figure 3-16.

query results consist of information from two tables

FIGURE 3-16

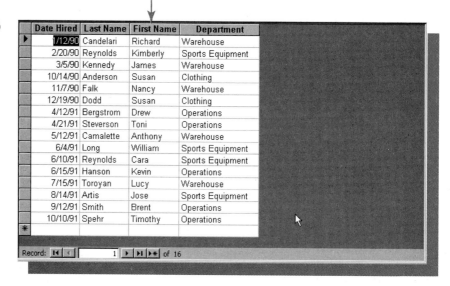

Date Hired	Last Name	First Name	Department
1/12/90	Candelari	Richard	Warehouse
2/20/90	Reynolds	Kimberly	Sports Equipment
3/5/90	Kennedy	James	Warehouse
10/14/90	Anderson	Susan	Clothing
11/7/90	Falk	Nancy	Warehouse
12/19/90	Dodd	Susan	Clothing
4/12/91	Bergstrom	Drew	Operations
4/21/91	Steverson	Toni	Operations
5/12/91	Camalette	Anthony	Warehouse
6/4/91	Long	William	Sports Equipment
6/10/91	Reynolds	Cara	Sports Equipment
6/15/91	Hanson	Kevin	Operations
7/15/91	Toroyan	Lucy	Warehouse
8/14/91	Artis	Jose	Sports Equipment
9/12/91	Smith	Brent	Operations
10/10/91	Spehr	Timothy	Operations

Record: ◄ ◄ 1 ► ►I ►* of 16

The query datasheet displays the same 16 records as in the original query, and in addition displays the Department field. Each record consists of information from both tables. Both tables must contain matching records in order for a record to appear in the query's result.

Next you want to change the order of the columns and sort the query datasheet by Department and Last Name.

■ Change the column order to Department, Last Name, First Name, and Date Hired.

■ Select the Department and Last Name columns.

■ Click [A↓] Sort Ascending.

Your screen should be similar to Figure 3-17.

fields in new order

Department	Last Name	First Name	Date Hired
Clothing	Anderson	Susan	10/14/90
Clothing	Dodd	Susan	12/19/90
Operations	Bergstrom	Drew	4/12/91
Operations	Hanson	Kevin	6/15/91
Operations	Smith	Brent	9/12/91
Operations	Spehr	Timothy	10/10/91
Operations	Steverson	Toni	4/21/91
Sports Equipment	Artis	Jose	8/14/91
Sports Equipment	Long	William	6/4/91
Sports Equipment	Reynolds	Cara	6/10/91
Sports Equipment	Reynolds	Kimberly	2/20/90
Warehouse	Camalette	Anthony	5/12/91
Warehouse	Candelari	Richard	1/12/90
Warehouse	Falk	Nancy	11/7/90
Warehouse	Kennedy	James	3/5/90
Warehouse	Toroyan	Lucy	7/15/91

Record: |◄| |◄| | 1 | |►| |►I| |►*| of 16

FIGURE 3-17

in ascending order sorted by department and last name

Saving a Query

You would like to save this query for the manager. You can save a query as an object, then you can run the query whenever needed. To do this,

- Choose File/Save As/Export.

- Type **Pre 1992 Hire Date**

- If necessary, select "Within the current database as."

- Click [OK].

You now have two named queries in the database: Hire Date and Pre 1992 Hire Date.

Querying Three Tables

Next the manager would like you to create some queries that will help in the analysis of the employee payroll information. The payroll information is in a table named Employee Pay Rates. This table contains the Employee ID and hourly pay rate.

You will create a query that will locate all employees hired after 11/15/93 and who work in the Clothing department. The manager would like the query to also display the employees' hourly rates. To create this query, you can modify the

existing query by adding the Employee Pay Rates table to the query design and
by changing the criteria.

The menu equivalent is **Q**uery/Show
T**a**ble.

- Return to the Query Design.

- Click  Show Table.

- Add the Employee Pay Rates table to the Query Design window.

- Close the Show Table dialog box.

Access automatically links
the Employee ID field of
the Employee Pay Rates
table to the Employees by
Department and Position
table.

Next you need to set up the criteria to display the requested information.

- Add the Hourly Rate field to the design grid.

- Replace the existing criterion in the Data Hired Criteria cell with
>11/15/93.

- Enter **"clothing"** as the criterion in the Department Criteria cell.

Field:	Date Hired	Last Name	First Name	Department	Hourly Rate
Table:	Sports Company Em	Sports Company Em	Sports Company Em	Employees by Depa	Employee Pay Ra
Sort:					
Show:	☑	☑	☑	☑	☑
Criteria:	>#11/15/93#			"clothing"	
or:					

Finally, you also want the query datasheet to display the records in alphabetical
order by last name. Another way to set the sort order is to specify the sort direction in the Sort cell of the grid.

- Move to the Sort cell of the Last Name field and open the drop-down list.

- Select Ascending.

- Run the query.

The query datasheet should be similar to Figure 3-18.

ascending sort order

FIGURE 3-18

Department	Last Name	First Name	Date Hired	Hourly Rate
Clothing	Adams	Bryan	6/3/97	$5.50
Clothing	Carrier	Kirk	3/2/97	$5.50
Clothing	Ehmann	Kurt	3/4/94	$10.50
Clothing	Fisher	Sarah	6/7/97	$5.00
Clothing	McKay	Ryan	6/15/96	$6.00
Clothing	McLean	Karen	8/15/96	$6.00
Clothing	Mitchell	Samuel	10/15/96	$6.00
Clothing	Morgan	Michael	10/15/96	$6.50
Clothing	Rawe	James	3/8/96	$6.00
Clothing	Richards	Patty	11/21/95	$11.00
Clothing	Rusher	Judi	1/2/97	$6.00
Clothing	Waxman	David	1/2/97	$5.50

query results including data from three tables

The query result shows, in alphabetical order by last name, the employees who were hired after 11/15/93 and work in the Clothing department. It also displays their hourly rate of pay.

The manager has also requested another list, sorted by Department, of all employees who earn less than $5.50 per hour. You will modify the query to display this information. In addition, since you no longer need the Date Hired field, you will remove it from the design grid.

- Return to Query Design view.

- Select the Date Hired column.

- Press Delete.

- Clear the criterion from the Department field.

- Enter the expression **<5.50** in the Hourly Rate Criteria cell.

- Set the Department sort order to Ascending

- Set the Last Name sort order to not sorted.

> Select a column by clicking on the column selector bar above the field name in the grid when the mouse pointer is ↓.

> The menu equivalent is **E**dit/Delete Colu**m**ns.

Field:	Date Hired
Table:	Sports Company Err

> Deleting a column from the design grid does not change the underlying table.

Last Name	First Name	Department	Hourly Rate
Sports Company Err	Sports Company Err	Employees by Depa	Employee Pay Rate
		Ascending	
☑	☑	☑	☑
			<5.5

- Run the query.

Your screen should be similar to Figure 3-19.

query results show employees earning less than $5.50 per hour
↓

FIGURE 3-19

Department	Last Name	First Name	Hourly Rate
Clothing	Fisher	Sarah	$5.00
Sports Equipment	Lawson	Tamara	$5.00
Sports Equipment	Moran	Jeannie	$5.00
Sports Equipment	Lye	Hin	$5.00
Warehouse	Castillo	Blas	$4.50
Warehouse	Lockwood	Craig	$5.25
Warehouse	Hayes	Carol	$5.00
Warehouse	Granger	Michael	$4.50
Warehouse	Jessup	Hart	$5.00
Warehouse	Fulton	Cindy	$5.00

The query datasheet shows that 10 employees earn less than $5.50.

Creating a Calculated Field

The manager reviewed the list of employees and has decided it is time to give these employees a raise. You have been asked to create a query that will calculate a 5 percent increase for these employees.

When creating queries you are not limited to just the fields in the database tables. You can also create fields based on information contained in other fields used in the query. This type of field is called a calculated field.

Concept 6: Calculated Field

A **calculated field** displays the result of a calculation in a query. You can perform a variety of calculations in queries. For example, you can calculate the sum of all inventory, the average salary for a department, or the highest sales figures among all sales personnel in the company. You can create your own calculation or use one of Access's seven predefined calculations shown below.

Predefined Calculation	What It Calculates
Sum	Totals values in a field for all records
Average	Averages values in a field for all records
Count	Counts number of values, excluding empty cells, in a field for all records
Minimum	Finds lowest value in a field for all records
Maximum	Finds highest value in a field for all records
Standard Deviation	A measure of the dispersion of a frequency distribution
Variance	Square of the standard deviation

To create a calculated field, you enter an expression in the design grid that instructs Access to perform a calculation using the current field values. Then the calculated result is displayed in the calculated field column of the datasheet.

To create a calculated field, you will enter the expression to perform the calculation in the Field row of a blank column

■ Return to the Query Design window.

■ Move to the Field row of a blank column.

You will need to enter a custom calculation to calculate the new pay rate for the records in the query. The first part of the expression will name the new calculated field. The second part of the expression does the actual calculation. In this case, to calculate the raise, the expression will multiply the value in the Hourly Rate field by 1.05 to calculate the 5 percent increase for each employee.

■ Type **New Rate:**

■ Press [Spacebar].

■ Type **[Hourly Rate]*1.05**

■ Press [←Enter].

■ Increase the column width to fully display the expression.

> New Rate: [Hourly Rate]*1.05

Before running the query, you would like to change the new field's properties so it will display the calculated values as currency with two decimal places.

■ Select the New Rate column.

■ Click [icon] Properties.

■ Select Currency from the Format drop-down list.

■ Close the Field Properties dialog box.

■ Run the query.

> Field names are enclosed in square brackets in an expression.

> If you made an entry error, a message box will appear advising you of the error. Clear the box and correct the expression.

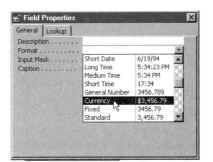

Your screen should be similar to Figure 3-20.

calculated field results displayed in currency format

Department	Last Name	First Name	Hourly Rate	New Rate
Clothing	Fisher	Sarah	$5.00	$5.25
Sports Equipment	Lawson	Tamara	$5.00	$5.25
Sports Equipment	Moran	Jeannie	$5.00	$5.25
Sports Equipment	Lye	Hin	$5.00	$5.25
Warehouse	Castillo	Blas	$4.50	$4.73
Warehouse	Lockwood	Craig	$5.25	$5.51
Warehouse	Hayes	Carol	$5.00	$5.25
Warehouse	Granger	Michael	$4.50	$4.73
Warehouse	Jessup	Hart	$5.00	$5.25
Warehouse	Fulton	Cindy	$5.00	$5.25

FIGURE 3-20

The query datasheet displays the 10 employees and shows their new pay rates in the last column. The New Rate column of values appears in the currency format you selected. You would like to save this query in case the manager wants to try different percent increases.

■ Save the query as **Pay Rate Increase**.

Finally, the manager has asked you to figure out what the average hourly rate is for all employees. Access can automatically make this calculation for you.

■ Switch to Query Design view.

■ Choose **Edit/Clear** Grid.

■ Add the Hourly Rate field back to the grid.

To calculate the average hourly rate, you need to display a new row called the Total row in the Design grid. The Total row is used to perform calculations such as a sum or average on values in one or more fields for all the records or a group of records in the query. The Total row is hidden by default. The $\boxed{\Sigma}$ Totals button toggles between hiding and displaying the row in the grid.

The menu equivalent is **View/Totals**.

■ Click $\boxed{\Sigma}$ Totals.

When calculating a total value, only one field, the field on which the calculation will be made, is displayed in the grid.

The Total row is displayed as the third row in the design grid. Every field in the grid must have a setting entered in the Total row. By default Access enters "Group By" as the setting. This setting is used to group data in the query. You need to change the setting to calculate the average of the Hourly Rate field.

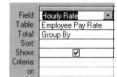

■ Move to the Total cell of the Hourly Rate column.

■ Select Avg from the Total drop-down list.

■ Run the query.

Your screen should be similar to Figure 3-21.

query result displays calculated average pay rate

FIGURE 3-21

When summary calculations are performed, the query result displays one record with a calculated value. In this case Access calculates $7.09 as the average rate of pay. You can now send this information along with the printout to the manager.

Querying Four Tables

The last query the manager requested will display the weekly gross pay for all employees sorted by department. To calculate the weekly gross pay, you will need to use the Weekly Hours Worked table, which contains the employee numbers along with the hours worked in the past weeks.

- Switch to the Query Design window.

- If necessary, maximize the window.

- Clear the grid.

- Hide the Total row.

- Add the Weekly Hours Worked table to the Query Design.

> Click Σ to hide the Total row.

This field list displays the fields Employee ID, Week Ending, and Hours. The table has been joined to the Employee Pay Rates table on the common field. Notice that Employee ID in this field list is not bold. When a field is bold, it indicates that it is a primary key field. Employee ID in this table is not a primary key field because there are multiple entries with the same numbers.

Next you will add the fields to be included in the query to the grid and create a calculated field to calculate the gross pay for the week ending 10/16/98.

- Add the Last Name, First Name, Department, and Week Ending fields to the design grid in that order.

- Sort the Department field in ascending order.

- Move to the field cell of a blank column.

- Type **Gross Pay: [Hourly Rate]*[Hours]**

- Press ⏎Enter.

- Set the Format property for the calculated field to display as currency.

- Enter the expression =**10/16/98** into the Week Ending Criteria cell.

- Clear the Show box for the Week Ending field so the date will not display in the query datasheet.

> Click on the Show box to clear the check box.

Your screen should be similar to Figure 3-22.

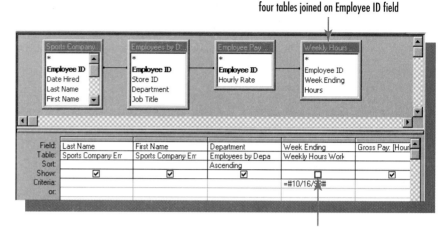

FIGURE 3-22

four tables joined on Employee ID field

clear Show box so field does not display in query result

■ Run the query.

Your screen should be similar to Figure 3-23.

gross pay for week of 10/16/98

FIGURE 3-23

Department	Last Name	First Name	Gross Pay
Clothing	McLean	Karen	$196.20
Clothing	Ehmann	Kurt	$367.50
Clothing	Morgan	Michael	$260.00
Clothing	Dodd	Susan	$220.50
Clothing	Rawe	James	$204.00
Clothing	Waxman	David	$192.50
Clothing	Richards	Patty	$440.00
Clothing	Mitchell	Samuel	$120.00
Clothing	Carrier	Kirk	$137.50
Clothing	Rusher	Judi	$240.00
Clothing	McKay	Ryan	$192.00
Clothing	Thorp	Blake	$262.50
Clothing	Adams	Bryan	$126.50
Clothing	Fisher	Sarah	$200.00
Clothing	Anderson	Susan	$197.60
Clothing	Nelson	Linda	$238.00
Operations	Steverson	Toni	$150.00
Operations	Abbott	Randal	$137.50

Record: |◄ ◄| 1 |► ►| ►*| of 73

The query datasheet displays the gross pay for each employee sorted by department for the week ending 10/16/98.

■ Print a copy of the query datasheet for the manager.

■ Save this query as **Gross Pay for 10/16/98**.

■ Close the Query Datasheet window.

■ Close the Employees by Department and Position table.

Creating a Multiple-Table Form

You have been using several tables of employee information that need to be up-dated each time information changes in an existing record. The form you cre-ated to use with the Sports Company Employees table can only update the records in that table. You want to create a form that will update the Sports Company Employees, Employee Pay Rates, and Employees by Department and Position tables. First you must create a query that will combine all the information you need, then you add the fields to the query that you want to display in the new form.

- ■ If necessary, open the Queries tab.

- ■ Choose [New] /Design View/[OK].

- ■ Add the Sports Company Employees, Employees by Department and Position, and Employee Pay Rates tables to the Query Design window.

- ■ Close the Show Table dialog box.

- ■ If necessary, maximize the Design View window.

- ■ From the Sports Company Employees table field list, add the following fields to the design grid in the order indicated (this will be the tab order on the form):

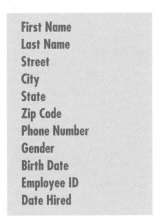

> **First Name**
> **Last Name**
> **Street**
> **City**
> **State**
> **Zip Code**
> **Phone Number**
> **Gender**
> **Birth Date**
> **Employee ID**
> **Date Hired**

> The fields continue to be added to the grid even though they are not all visible onscreen. Use the scroll bar to move to the other fields.

- ■ From the Employees by Department and Position table, add the following fields to the query design grid:

> **Store ID**
> **Department**
> **Job Title**

- ■ From the Employee Pay Rates table, add the Hourly Rate field to the design grid.

Your screen should be similar to Figure 3-24.

FIGURE 3-24

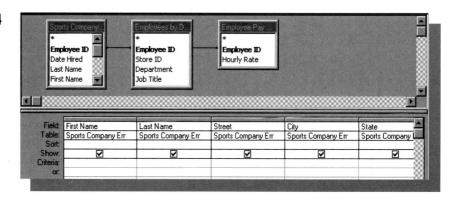

■ Save the query as **Comprehensive Employee Query**.

■ Close the Query Design window.

You are now ready to create the new form based on the Comprehensive Employee Query you just created. The form will include all fields in the query. You will use a columnar form style.

> Although you can create a form from scratch using Design view, it is much easier to create the form using a Wizard and then modify it in Form Design view.

■ Open the Forms tab.

■ Choose [New]/Form Wizard.

■ Click [OK].

■ Select Comprehensive Employee Query from the Table/Queries drop-down list.

■ Click [>>].

■ Click [Next >].

■ Click [Next >].

> This text will use Evergreen.

■ Select a style of your choice.

■ Click [Next >].

■ Enter the form title **Employee Update Form**.

■ Click [Finish].

After a few moments, the Form window displays the form in the selected style and layout. Next you want to modify the layout of the Form.

■ Click [▨] Design.

■ If necessary, maximize the window.

■ Rearrange the controls as in Figure 3-25.

■ Enter the form title and section headings shown in Figure 3-25.

- Set the font size of all controls to 10 and size the controls as appropriate.

- Set the title font to 20, size the control to fit, and add color.

- Set the Personal Data and Company Data font size to 12, size the controls to fit, and add color.

- Adjust the spacing and alignment of controls appropriately.

Your screen should be similar to Figure 3-25.

FIGURE 3-25

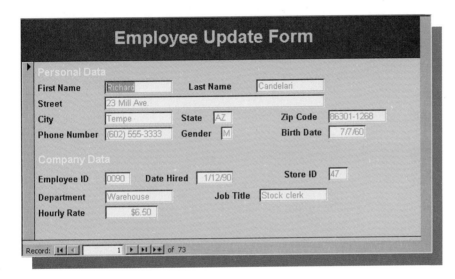

Next you want to add transparent rectangles around the controls in the Personal Data and Company Data sections of the form. To create the rectangle around the Personal Data section of the form first,

- Click [ ] Rectangle.

- Drag to create a box around the controls as you did to select multiple controls.

- Click [ ] Fill/Back Color.

- Select Transparent.

- Click [ ] Line/Border Width.

- Click [2].

- Click [ ] Line Border Color.

- Select the same color as the titles.

Your screen should be similar to Figure 3-26.

FIGURE 3-26

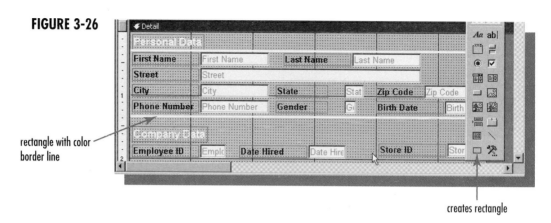

rectangle with color
border line

creates rectangle

- Create a second rectangle around the Company Data section of the form using the same settings.

- Adjust the rectangles so they are the same width.

- When you are done, view the form in Form view.

Your screen should be similar to Figure 3-27.

FIGURE 3-27

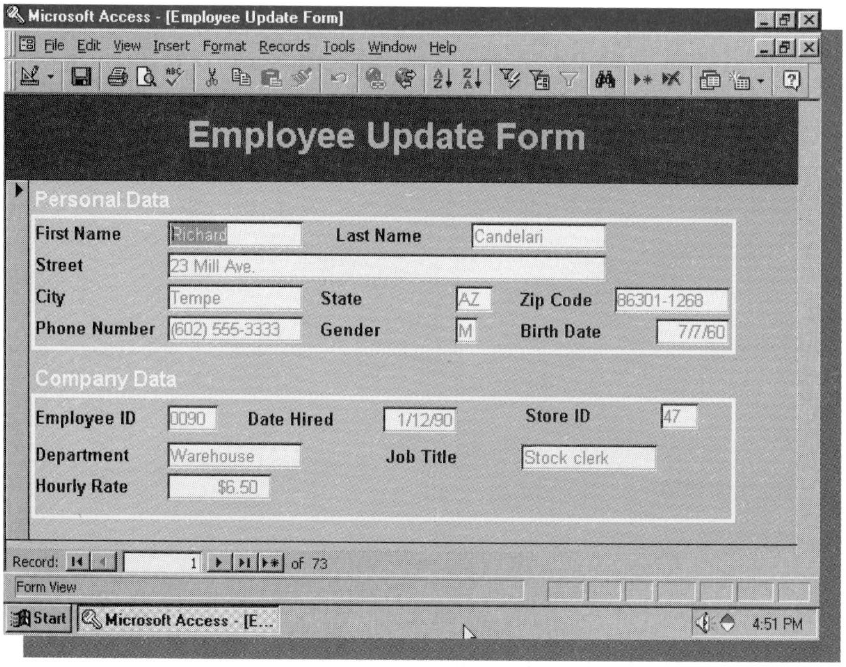

- To see how quickly the form can be used to update all three files, you will make several changes in the data to your record.

- Use the Find Records command to quickly display the record containing your information.

- Change the data in the following fields:

Field	Data
Zip Code	85000-0000
Store ID	68
Hourly Rate	9.75

Use [Tab] to move between fields in the form.

- Select your record and print the form with your record information displayed.

- Close the form, saving your layout changes.

- To verify that the changes were made to the tables, open each of the tables, locate your record, and note the changes.

As you can see, using a single customized form to update records in all three tables simultaneously is a great time-saving feature.

- Close the open tables, saving any changes.

- Exit Access, responding Yes to any prompt to save.

LAB REVIEW

Key Terms

calculated field   (DB124)
cell   (DB111)
column selector bar   (DB111)
comparison operator   (DB111)
criteria   (DB100)
criteria expression   (DB102)
design grid   (DB111)
field list   (DB111)
filter   (DB100)
Filter by Form   (DB101)
Filter by Selection   (DB100)
inner join   (DB118)
join   (DB118)
many-to-many relationship   (DB118)

multitable query   (DB116)
one-to-many relationship   (DB118)
one-to-one relationship   (DB118)
query   (DB107)
query datasheet   (DB109)
referential integrity (DB118)
relationship   (DB118)
wildcard character   (DB105)

Command Summary

Command	Shortcut	Toolbar	Action
File/SaveAs/Export			Saves a database object with a new name
Edit/Delete Columns	Delete		Removes selected column from design grid
Edit/Clear Grid		✕	Clears all fields from filter form or query design grid
View/Totals		Σ	Displays/hides Total row in query design grid
Records/Filter/Filter by Selection		▽	Displays only records that contain a specific value
Records/Filter/Filter by Form		▦	Displays blank datasheet for entering values to be displayed
Tools/Relationships			Defines permanent relationship between tables
Filter/Apply Filter/Sort		▽	Applies filter to table
Query/Run		!	Displays query results in Query Datasheet view
Query/Show Table		▦	Displays Show Table dialog box
Window/1 <name>			Displays selected window
		▦	Displays Database window

Matching

1. !	_____	**a.**	intersection of a column and row
2. query	_____	**b.**	matches any single character
3. multitable query	_____	**c.**	temporary restriction placed on displayed data to isolate specific records
4. criteria	_____	**d.**	includes any records containing either condition
5. ▦	_____	**e.**	symbols used to represent unknown characters in expressions
6. filter	_____	**f.**	runs a query and displays query datasheet
7. OR operator	_____	**g.**	used to ask questions about database tables
8. wildcard operator	_____	**h.**	query that uses data from more than one table
9. ?	_____	**i.**	set of limiting conditions
10. cell	_____	**j.**	accesses Filter By Form feature

Fill-In Questions

1. A(n) _____ is used to isolate and display a specific group of records.

2. The _____ operator narrows the search for records that meet both conditions.

3. Placeholders called _____ are used to specify a value when you want to find all values that begin with a specific character.

4. _____ is an association that shows how data between tables is related.

5. A(n) _____ retrieves specific data from one or more tables and displays the results in a query datasheet.

6. The _____ of the Query window is where the fields to be displayed in the query datasheet are placed.

7. Tables are joined by defining a(n) _____ between the tables.

8. A(n) _____ relationship is only possible if there is a junction table between the two tables.

9. The _____ row is used to perform calculations on all the values in a field.

10. In expressions field names are enclosed in _____.

Discussion Questions

1. Discuss what filters are and how they can be used in a database. When would it be appropriate to use a filter?

2. Discuss the differences between the AND and OR filter conditions.

3. Describe the six wildcard characters that are available in Access. Give an example of each.

4. Discuss what a query can do and some advantages of using queries.

5. Discuss the three types of relationships. Give an example of how an inner join could be created in a database.

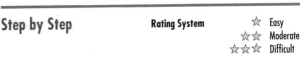

Hands-On Practice Exercises

	Rating System		
Step by Step		☆	Easy
		☆☆	Moderate
		☆☆☆	Difficult

1. This problem is a continuation of Practice Exercise 4 in Lab 2. Debbie from Desert Rescue Cleaning Service wants you to help her use her database to make management decisions concerning her growing business. She needs to be able to compare rates by square feet among all of her clients, wants to identify her largest clients, and wants you to create a query that she can refer back to as her business grows to track total square feet cleaned and total income.

a. Open the Desert Rescue Cleaning Service database. Filter the Clients table to display only those clients with 10,000 square feet or more. Print the filtered datasheet. Remove the filter.

b. Next, help Debbie create a new query based on the Clients table. Add the Company, Square Feet, and Rate fields to the design grid. Run the query, then print the query datasheet.

c. Debbie is pleased with the data you were able to extract for her. Now she wants to know which clients have at least 10,000 square feet of space. Return to Query Design view, then add the expression >=10000 in the Square Ft Criteria cell. Run the query, then print the query datasheet.

d. Debbie now wants a query, which she plans to use repeatedly, that will give her a summary of the size of her jobs and her expected income. Return to Query Design view, remove the criterion in the Square Ft column, then remove the Company field. Display the Total row in the design grid. Display the Total drop-down list and replace Group By with Sum in both fields in the grid. Run the query, then print the query datasheet. Save the query as Square Feet and Rates Totals.

DATABASE

2. This problem is a continuation of Practice Exercise 3 in Lab 2. Eddie Fitzpatrick of TechnoBabble Electronics wants you to help him check his inventory and print a list of inventory supplied by his favorite supplier. Eddie is also working with his local bank to secure a small business loan and wants you to help him find the total value of each item in inventory.

a. Open the TechnoBabble Electronics database and the Inventory table. Filter the table to display only those records where the number on hand is less than 5. Print the filtered datasheet. Remove the filter. Close the Inventory table.

b. Open the TechnoBabble Electronics Inventory List form and add the following new records to the inventory:

	Record 1	Record 2
Item #:	5396	5837
Description:	Calculator, Desktop	Projector, Computer Display
Shelf:	L-10	P-17
# On Hand:	10	2
Purchase Price:	$24.60	$1123.25
Supplier:	BTO	BTO
Status:	STOCK	SPECORDER
Cost:	$15.00	$797.15

c. Next you will query the table to display a list of inventory items from his favorite supplier, Business Technology Originators, with the supplier code BTO. Create a new query based on the Inventory table, then add the Item #, Description, and Supplier fields to the design grid. Enter the criteria to display all records that have BTO as the supplier. Clear the Show box of the Supplier field. Run the query. Print the query datasheet.

d. Now you will help Eddie get the inventory totals for his bank loan officer. You will need to know the number on hand of each item and the item's cost to TechnoBabble to calculate the total value of each item. Delete the Supplier column from the design grid, then add the # On Hand and Cost fields to the grid. To calculate the total value of each item, enter

the expression Total Value: [Cost]*[# On Hand]. Set the format of the calculated field to currency. Run the query, then print the query datasheet.

e. So that Eddie can track the total value of his inventory as he buys and sells items, save the query as Inventory Value.

3. This problem is a continuation of Practice Exercise 2 in Lab 2. Michelle at Food for Thought has been updating her database, and has added a table that tracks billing by client number. Michelle recently spoke with Debbie at Desert Rescue Cleaning Service about the queries you helped Debbie create. Michelle needs the same kind of analysis of her own clients and wants you to help her find clients who had at least one party that cost more than $1000 during 1995.

a. Open Updated Catering Records, the database that contains Michelle's updated records for Food for Thought. Create a new query based on the Billing table, then add the Customer #, Amount, and Invoice Date fields to the design grid. To indicate invoices of more than $1000 for 1995, enter >1000 in the Criteria cell of the Amount column and >=1/1/95 AND <=12/31/95 in the Invoice Date column. Run the query.

b. Michelle realizes that the query datasheet is not really useful without the customer names. Return to Query Design view and add the Customers table to the Query window. Add the Company field to the design grid, then run the query.

c. Michelle now has the information she needs in the query datasheet, but would prefer that the company name be displayed between the Customer # and Amount columns. Move the Company column to the new location, then print the query datasheet and close the Query window without saving the query.

d. You are about to leave when Michelle remembers that she got a good buy on beans and wants to find out which customers like baked beans. Use a filter to display only those customers who prefer baked beans. Print the filtered datasheet. Then remove the filter and close the table.

On Your Own

4. This problem is a continuation of Practice Exercise 1 in Lab 2. James O'Dell needs to gather data about his store inventory. He wants to gather information about a series of item numbers that he fears may be overstocked. In addition, he would like to see the value of each item in stock.

Open the Valley of the Sun Office Supplies database, then create a new query to display all records where the item numbers begin with either a 2 or a 3. Include appropriate fields in the query. Run the query and print the query datasheet.

James wants more detailed information about the items you located in the first query. He wants to know which items begin with either a 2 or a 3 and have more than 40 items on hand. Run the query and print the query datasheet.

James has almost all the information he needs, but he would like to see dollar amounts for each item. Calculate the total value of each item in the query datasheet. Run the new query and print the query datasheet.

Save the query as Overstocked Items and close the Query window.

5. This problem is a continuation of Practice Exercise 5 in Lab 2. Now that you are on staff at the Go West Dude Ranch, Michael wants you to add some capabilities to his payroll records. You have already created a new table, called Time Card, that tracks weekly hours worked. Next you will add a field to the Staff Records table to track salaries. You will also create a form for the new table you created. Finally, you will create queries for figuring the weekly paychecks for each employee.

Open the Dude Ranch Payroll database with the updated records, then add the Pay Rate field to the Staff Records table. Format the field to display as currency.

Enter the following pay rates for each employee in the Staff Records table:

Employee #	Pay Rate
015	$12.50
131	6.75
139	8.25
216	4.75
275	4.75

Due to a data processing error, your personal information was lost. Reenter your data, including a pay rate for yourself and an employee number.

Your updated database includes a Time Card table that tracks weekly hours worked by each employee. Create a columnar form based on the Time Card table and name the form Weekly Time Card. Use the new Weekly Time Card form to enter data for the current week:

Employee #	Hours Worked
015	40
131	38
139	27.25
216	40
275	20
Your #	Your Hours

Now you need to create a new query that will figure paychecks for all employees. Create a multitable query to display the pay rate and total hours worked for each employee during the current week. You will also need to calculate the gross pay for each employee. Format the gross pay field to currency. Print the query datasheet, then save the query as Weekly Paychecks.

6. This problem is a continuation of Practice Exercise 6 in Lab 2.

Open the My Contacts database and create a query to display company name, contact, and phone number for all records. Print the query datasheet.

Open the form you created in Lab 2. Change the form colors and fonts to make it easier to read and more attractive. Print one record in the revised form. Save any changes to your form.

Create at least two other queries of the data in your table that you can use to analyze the data. Print the query results.

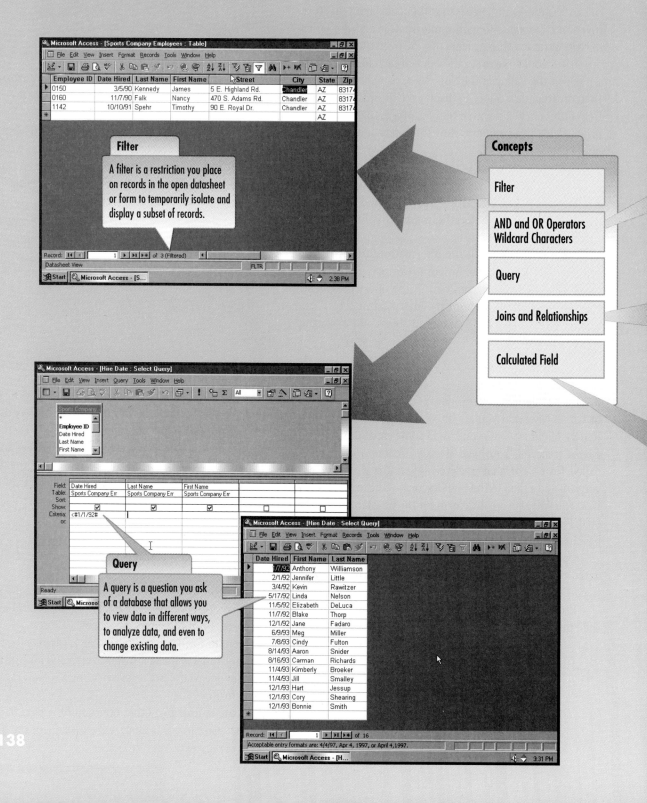

Filter

A filter is a restriction you place on records in the open datasheet or form to temporarily isolate and display a subset of records.

Concepts

- Filter
- AND and OR Operators Wildcard Characters
- Query
- Joins and Relationships
- Calculated Field

Query

A query is a question you ask of a database that allows you to view data in different ways, to analyze data, and even to change existing data.

AND and OR Operators

The AND and OR operators are used to specify multiple conditions that must be met for the records to display in the datasheet.

Wildcard Characters

Wildcard characters are placeholders that represent any series of characters or any single character.

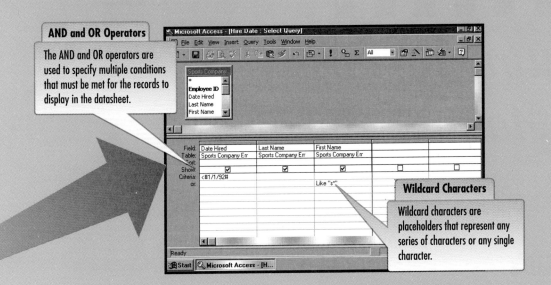

Joins and Relationships

You can bring information from different tables in your database together by defining a relationship to join the tables.

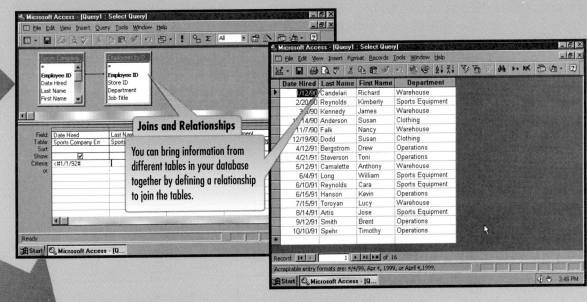

Calculated Field

A calculated field displays the result of a calculation in a query.

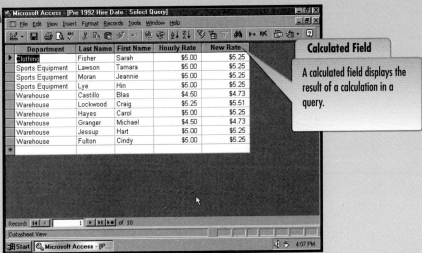

Creating Reports and Mailing Labels

CASE STUDY

The manager is impressed with your ability to use Access to quickly locate and analyze the data in the employee tables. You have used the program to automate the daily updates and changes that occur to the employee tables and to quickly find answers to many different types of queries. The printed output of the query results is a simple report that is acceptable for many informal uses.

Next you have been asked to create weekly and monthly employee status reports. You want these reports to have a more professional appearance suitable for a formal report or presentation. You will create several reports that group and summarize the data in an organized and attractive manner. An example of one of the reports you will create is shown at right.

Finally, you have been asked to create mailing labels from the employee database. One page of the labels you will create is shown below.

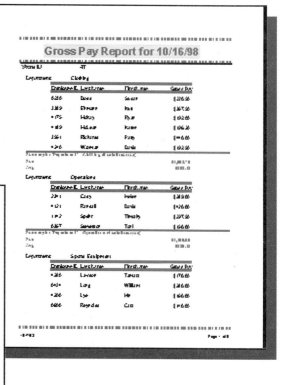

Concept Overview

The following concepts will be introduced in this lab:

1. Reports	Reports are the printed output you generate from tables or queries.
2. Grouping Records	Records in a report can be grouped into categories to allow you to better analyze the data.
3. Group Calculations	If you group data in your report, you can perform calculations on values, such as a group total, an average, a minimum value, and a maximum value.
4. Layout Preview	Layout Preview displays a sample of the data in the report so you can quickly check the report's layout.

Part 1

Using the AutoReport Wizard

The manager would like a report that displays the employees' names and addresses ordered by name. You have already created and printed several simple reports using the Print command on the File menu. This time, however, you want to create a custom report of this information.

Concept 1: Reports

Access **reports** are the printed output you generate from tables or queries. It might be a simple listing of all the fields in a table, or it might be a list of selected fields based on a query.

Access also includes a custom report feature that allows you to create professional-appearing reports. The custom report is a document that includes text formats, styles, and layouts that enhance the display of information. In addition, you can group data in reports to achieve specific results. You can then display summary information, such as totals, by group to allow the reader to further analyze the data. Creating a custom report displays the information from your database in a more attractive and meaningful format.

You will create the address list report using the data in the Sports Company Employees table in the Sports Company Personnel Records database.

- Load Access 97. Put your data disk in drive A (or the appropriate drive for your system).

Use the Sports Company Personnel Records database from the end of Lab 3.

- Open the Sports Company Personnel Records database file.

- Open the Reports tab.

The menu equivalent is Insert/Report.

- Click ▐ New ▐.

The New Report dialog box on your screen should be similar to Figure 4-1.

FIGURE 4-1

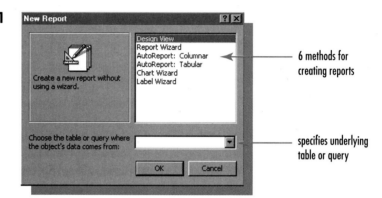

The dialog box presents six ways to create a report. You can create a report from scratch in Design view, or by using the Report Wizard or one of the AutoReport Wizards. The Report Wizard lets you choose the fields to include in the report and it helps you quickly format and lay out the new report. The AutoReport Wizard creates a report that displays all fields and records from the underlying table or query in a predesigned report layout and style.

You decide to use the AutoReport Wizard to create a columnar report using data in the Sports Company Employees table.

- Select AutoReport: Columnar.

- Select Sports Company Employees from the Choose the Table or Query drop-down list.

- Click ▐ OK ▐.

After a few moments, the report is created and displayed in the Print Preview window.

- To see more of the report, maximize the window.

Your screen should be similar to Figure 4-2.

Zoom button

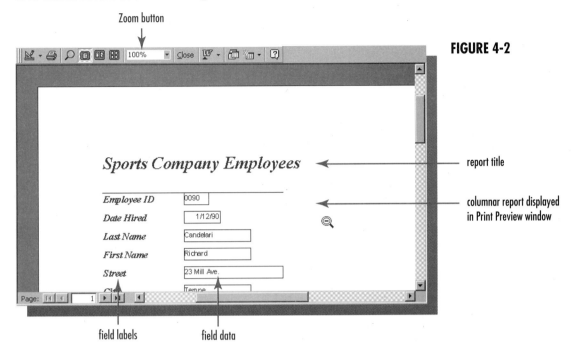

FIGURE 4-2

report title

columnar report displayed
in Print Preview window

field labels   field data

The AutoReport Wizard creates a columnar report that displays each field on a
separate line in a single column for each record. The fields are in the order they
appear in the table. The report appears in a predefined report style and layout.
The report style shown in Figure 4-2 uses the table name as the report title and
includes the use of text colors, typefaces and sizes, and horizontal lines and boxes.

Your report may be displayed with a different style. This is because when
creating an AutoReport, Access remembers the last autoformat report style used
to create a report, then applies that same style to the new report. If the Autoformat
command has not been used, the report will use the basic style. You will learn
how to change styles later in this lab.

Zooming the Window

Only the upper part of the first page of the report is visible in the window. To see
more of the report in the window at one time, you can decrease the onscreen
character size by specifying a smaller magnification percentage using the Zoom
command. The default magnification percentage of 100% is displayed in the
Zoom toolbar button. This setting shows the characters the same size as they
will be when printed. You can increase the character size up to two times normal
display (200%) or reduce it to 10%.

- Open the 100% ▼ Zoom Control drop-down list.

- Choose 50%.

The Zoom feature is available in all Print
Preview windows.

The menu equivalent is **V**iew/**Z**oom/50%.

The text is reduced in size by half, allowing you to view more of the page in the window. You can now see three sides of the page. You can further adjust the magnification to display the whole page in the window using the Fit option.

The menu equivalent is **V**iew/**Z**oom/**F**it to Window.

■ Choose Fit from the Zoom drop-down list.

Your screen should be similar to Figure 4-3.

FIGURE 4-3

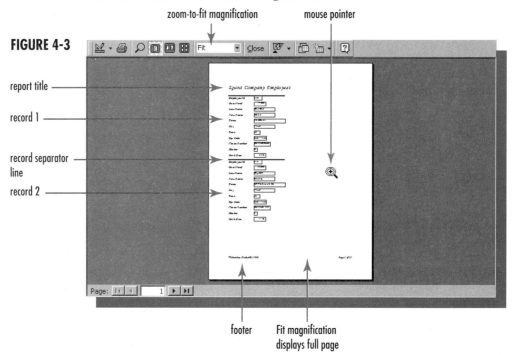

zoom-to-fit magnification   mouse pointer

report title

record 1

record separator line

record 2

footer   Fit magnification displays full page

Now the entire page is visible, but most of the text is too small to read. However, you can now see the entire page layout. The report title appears at the top of the page, and each field of information is displayed on a separate line in a single column for each record. Each record is separated from the next by a horizontal line. The current date and page number appear at the bottom of the page in the footer. The first two records from the Sports Company Employees table are displayed on the first page of the report.

Just as in Table, Form, and Datasheet views, you can use the navigation keys and navigation buttons to move through the pages of the report.

Notice that the mouse pointer is a ⊕ when it is positioned on the page. This indicates that you can you can switch between the last magnification level you set and the Fit magnification by clicking on the report. The location of the pointer on the report when you click indicates the area of the report that will appear in the window.

You can also click ⊘ Zoom in the toolbar to zoom in and out.

■ With the mouse pointer as ⊕, click on the report title.

The **V**iew/P**a**ges command can be used to display up to 12 pages, and the ⊞ button can be used to display up to 20 pages of a report in the window.

The page is displayed at 50% magnification again. You can also view multiple report pages at the same time in Print Preview. To view six pages,

■ Click ⊞ Multiple Pages.

■ Drag to select six pages (2x3).

Use ⊟ to quickly display two pages and ⊡ to display a single page.

Your screen should be similar to Figure 4-4.

displays multiple pages

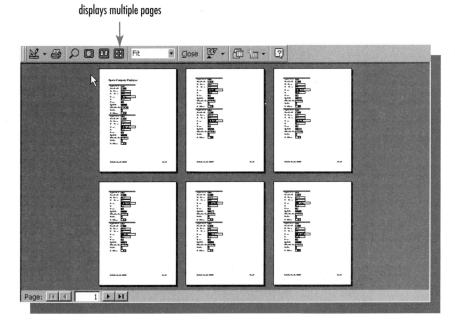

FIGURE 4-4

After looking over the columnar report, you decide the layout is inappropriate for your report because only two records are printed per page, making the report larger than 50 pages. In addition, you do not want the report to include all the fields from the table. To close the report file without saving it,

■ Click ☒.

■ Click No .

> Do not click Close on the toolbar. This closes the Print Preview window, but does not close the report file.

Using the Report Wizard

You want the report to display the field contents for each record on a line rather than in a column. You also want to display the employee name and address information only. The Report Wizard will create this type of report. From the Reports tab,

■ Choose New /Report Wizard/ OK .

The Report Wizard consists of a series of dialog boxes, much like the Form Wizard. In the first dialog box (see Figure 4-5) you specify the table or query to be used in the report and select the fields.

■ Select Table: Sports Company Employees from the Tables/Queries drop-down list.

■ Add the fields to the Selected Fields list in the following order:

> First Name
> Last Name
> Street
> City
> State
> Zip Code

Fields are added just as in Form Wizard.

The fields appear in the report in the order in which you place them in the Selected Fields list.

You do not have to include all the fields in the table on a report.

The Report Wizard dialog box on your screen should be similar to Figure 4-5.

fields that will appear in report

FIGURE 4-5

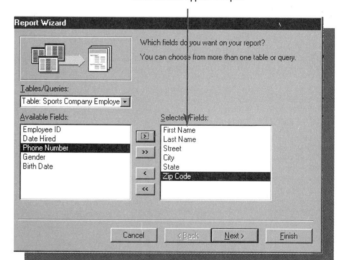

■ Click Next >.

You will learn about grouping later in this lab.

In the second Report Wizard dialog box you specify how to group the data in the report. The manager does not want the report grouped by any category. To move to the next dialog box,

■ Click Next >.

The next dialog box (see Figure 4-6) is used to specify a sort order for the records. A report can be sorted on up to four fields. The manager would like the report sorted in ascending order by last name and by first name within same last names.

■ Select Last Name from the number 1 drop-down list and First Name from the number 2 drop-down list.

Clicking [A↓] toggles between ascending and descending sort order.

The default order of ascending for both fields is appropriate.

The dialog box on your screen should be similar to Figure 4-6.

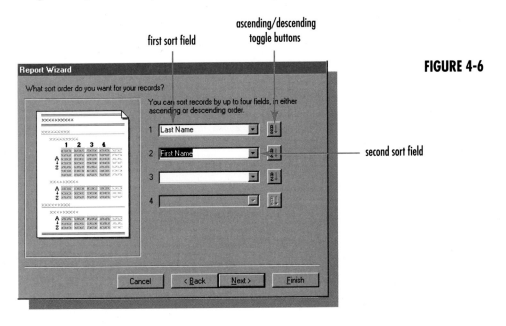

FIGURE 4-6

■ Click [Next >]

The next dialog box is used to change the report layout and orientation. The default report settings create a tabular layout using portrait orientation. In addition, the option to adjust the field width so all fields fit on one page is selected. Because this report is very wide, the only change you will make is to change the orientation to landscape.

■ Select **L**andscape.

■ Click [Next >]

From this dialog box you select a style for the report. The preview area displays a sample of each style as it is selected. You believe the Bold style is most appropriate for this report.

■ Select each style to preview the style options.

■ Select Bold.

■ Click [Next >]

The last Report Wizard dialog box is used to add a title to the report and to specify how the report should be displayed after it is created. The only change you want to make is to replace the table name with a more descriptive report title.

■ Type **Employee Address Report**

■ Click [**F**inish]

The program takes a minute to generate the report, during which time Report Design view is briefly displayed. In a few moments, the completed report with the data from the underlying table is displayed in the Print Preview window.
Your screen should be similar to Figure 4-7.

FIGURE 4-7

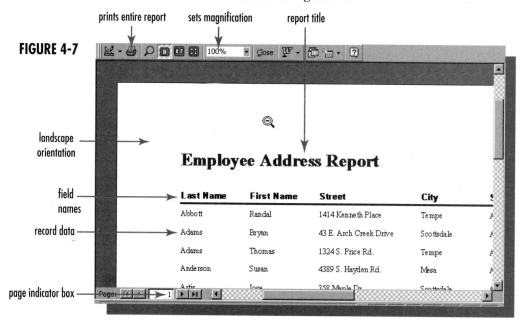

The Print Preview window displays the first page of the report in landscape orientation using the selected Bold report style. The report title reflects the title you specified using the Wizard. The names of the selected fields are displayed on the first line of the report and each record appears on a separate row below the field names. Notice that the Last Name field is the first field, even though you selected it as the second field. This is because the sort order overrides the selected field order.

- Change the magnification to Fit.

You can now see the layout of the report on the entire page. The address information easily fits across the page with the orientation set to landscape. You like the layout of this report and do not need to make any changes to the report design. Next you will print the page containing your record.

Increase the magnification to locate your record more easily.

- Move to the page of the report that contains your name.

- Choose **F**ile/**P**rint.

The page number is displayed in the page indicator box.

- If necessary, select the appropriate printer for your system.

- Select Pa**g**es.

- Type the page number containing your record in the From and To text boxes.

The 🖶 Print button prints the entire report.

- Click ▭ OK ▭.

- Close the Employee Address Report file.

The Database window is displayed again, and the report object name is listed in the Reports object list. The Report Wizard automatically saves the report using the report title as the object name.

Creating a Report from a Query

The next report you want to create will display the employees' gross pay grouped by store and department. You have sketched out the report to look like the one shown below.

```
                    Gross Pay Report for xx/xx/xx


    Store ID:  XX
    Department:          XXXXXXXX


    Employee ID      Last Name       First Name      Gross Pay

    XXXXXXXX         XXXXXXX         XXXXX           $XXXX.XX
    XXXXXXXX         XXXXXXX         XXXXX           $XXXX.XX


    Sum by Dept.                                     $XXXXX.XX
    Avg by Dept.                                     $XXXXX.XX
    Sum by Store                                     $XXXXX.XX
    Avg by Store                                     $XXXXX.XX
```

To create this report, you will use the query you created in Lab 3 and saved as Gross Pay for 10/16/98. It is usually helpful to run the query first to remind you of the data that the query gathers.

■ From the Queries tab, open the Gross Pay for 10/16/98 query.

The query datasheet displays the Department, Last Name, First Name, and Gross Pay fields. In addition, you need the report to display the Employee ID and the Store ID fields. To include these fields in the report, you need to add them to the query design grid.

■ Switch to Query Design view.

■ Add the Employee ID and Store ID fields to the design grid.

■ Run the query.

■ Arrange the field columns so Store ID is the second column and Employee ID is the third column.

■ Clear the highlight.

> If you create a report based on multiple tables, the relationship between tables must be established first using **T**ools/ **R**elationships.

Your screen should be similar to Figure 4-8.

FIGURE 4-8

Department	Store ID	Employee ID	Last Name	First Name	Gross Pay
Clothing	47	4189	McLean	Karen	$196.20
Clothing	47	3389	Ehmann	Kurt	$367.50
Clothing	52	4211	Morgan	Michael	$260.00
Clothing	47	0230	Dodd	Susan	$220.50
Clothing	52	4132	Rawe	James	$204.00
Clothing	47	4240	Waxman	David	$192.50
Clothing	47	3561	Richards	Patty	$440.00
Clothing	57	4208	Mitchell	Samuel	$120.00
Clothing	68	4255	Carrier	Kirk	$137.50
Clothing	57	4239	Rusher	Judi	$240.00
Clothing	47	4175	McKay	Ryan	$192.00
Clothing	52	1473	Thorp	Blake	$262.50
Clothing	57	4282	Adams	Bryan	$126.50
Clothing	57	4310	Fisher	Sarah	$200.00
Clothing	52	0151	Anderson	Susan	$197.60
Clothing	57	1388	Nelson	Linda	$238.00
Operations	47	0367	Steverson	Toni	$150.00
Operations	68	4281	Abbott	Randal	$137.50

Record: 1 of 73

new fields added to query

Now you are ready to create a report using the data from the query. Rather than switching to the Report tab of the Database window and choosing New, you can use the ▦▾ New Object button to create a new object of any type.

- Open the ▦▾ New Object drop-down list.

- Select Report.

- If you are prompted to save the query, click [Yes].

The New Report dialog box correctly displays the name of the selected query as the object on which the report will be based.

- Choose Report Wizard/[OK].

The Available Fields list box displays the fields that are included in the design grid in the Gross Pay for 10/16/98 query. You want to include all the fields in the report.

- Click [>>].

- Click [Next >].

Grouping a Report

In the next dialog box you need to select the fields on which you want to group the report.

Concept 2: Grouping Records

Records in a report can be **grouped** by categories to allow you to better analyze the data. It is often helpful to group records and calculate totals for the entire group. For example, it might be useful for a store manager to group payroll records by department. Then, rather than getting a long list of pay for individual employees, the manager could get a report showing total payroll for each department. A mail order company might group orders by date of purchase, then by item number to see detailed sales information.

In Access you can create a report that will automatically group records based on fields you choose to group by. You can group by up to 10 fields in any one report.

Groups should be created based on priority from the largest to smallest. To group the report by store number and then by department within store number,

> The Priority buttons can be used to change the grouping order of priority.

■ Select Store ID.

■ Click [>].

■ Select Department.

■ Click [>].

The dialog box on your screen should be similar to Figure 4-9.

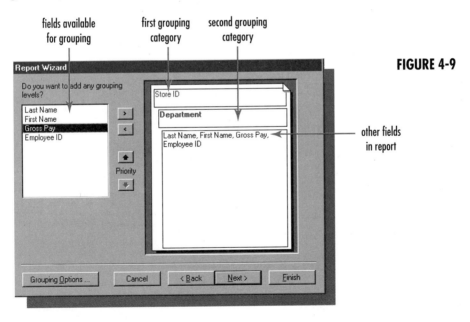

FIGURE 4-9

■ Click [Next >].

In this dialog box you specify a sort order for the data grouped within each field. In addition, because you have specified groups, you can also include calculations to summarize the grouped data.

Concept 3: Group Calculations

If you group data in your report, you can perform one or more of the following calculations on values: Sum (adds all values by group), Avg (calculates the average value for the group), Min (calculates the lowest value for the group), and Max (calculates the highest value for the group).

You can select multiple calculations to complete different analyses of the data. For example, a mail order company might calculate the sum of different products sold on each day of the month and the average sale for each day. You can also calculate the percent of total for the sums. For example, the mail order company might want to know what percentage of total sales were made on a specific product for June 15.

You can further customize the report to display both detailed information and the summary information, or just the summary information while hiding the details about the individual items.

You would like the report sorted by last name and then by first name, and to display a total and average for each department and store.

- Select Last Name as the first field to sort on and First Name as the second field to sort on.

- Click Summary Options ....

- Select Sum.

- Select Avg.

- Click OK.

- Click Next >.

The dialog box on your screen should be similar to Figure 4-10.

sample of selected layout   available layouts   page orientation

FIGURE 4-10

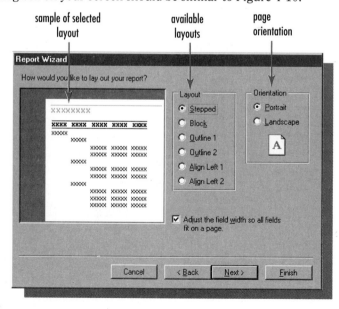

In this dialog box you are asked to select from six different layout options for a grouped report. You will use the Outline 1 layout.

- Select each layout option and look at the sample previews.

- Select **O**utline 1.

- Click Next > .

From the last two Report Wizard dialog boxes, you will select the report style and enter the title.

- Select Casual.

- Click Next > .

- Edit the report title to be **Gross Pay Report for 10/16/98**.

- Click Finish .

- Set the Print Preview window magnification to 75%.

Your screen should be similar to Figure 4-11.

FIGURE 4-11

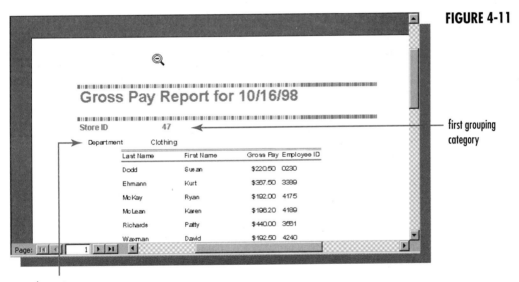

first grouping category

second grouping category

The data in the report is grouped by store and department, and the records are alphabetized by last name within groups. The information for store 47 is the first store group, and the Clothing department is the department group within the store group.

- Scroll the report to see the summary data at the bottom of the Clothing group.

In addition, each department group displays a count of employees and the sum and average values below the Gross Pay data column.

- Display page 2 and, if necessary, scroll the report to see the information at the end of the store 47 group and the beginning of the store 52 group.

Your screen should be similar to Figure 4-12.

FIGURE 4-12

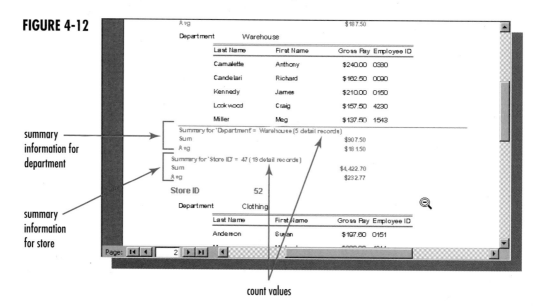

summary information for department

summary information for store

count values

The summary information for store 47 appears above the Store 52 group head. It includes a count value, and total and average gross pay values for the store.

- ■ Display the top of the last page of the report.

A grand total value for all stores appears at the end of the report.

- ■ Display the top of page 1 again.

Note: If you are ending your session now, close the Report file and exit Access. When you begin Part 2, open the Sports Company Personnel Records database file. Then Preview the Gross Pay Report for 10/16/98.

Part 2

Modifying the Report Design

As you looked through the report, you saw several changes you wanted to make. The first change is to rearrange the order of the fields in the report and to size the fields appropriately. In addition, you want to make the store group head more noticeable, to change the display of the date in the footer to exclude the day of the week, and to center the title over the report. Report Design view is used to modify the appearance of the report.

- ■ Click 🔲 Report Design.
- ■ If necessary, move the Toolbox to the right border of the window.

Your screen should be similar to Figure 4-13.

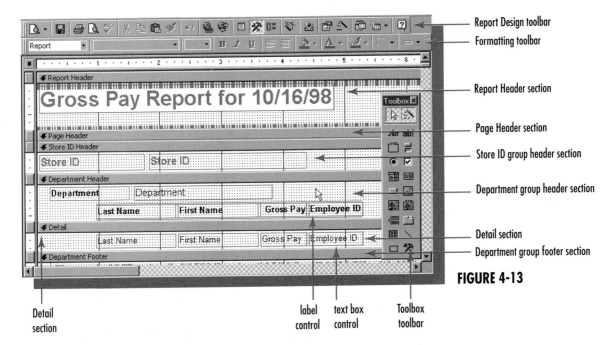

FIGURE 4-13

As you can see, Report Design view is very similar to Form Design view. It displays horizontal and vertical rulers to help with the placement of controls on the grid. It also displays three toolbars: Report Design, Formatting, and Toolbox. The Formatting and Toolbox toolbars are the same as in Form view. The Report Design toolbar contains the standard buttons as well as buttons (identified below) that are specific to the Report Design view window.

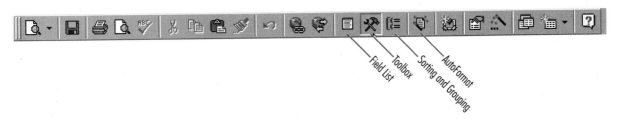

Some sections may not be currently visible in the Report Design window.

The Report Design view window consists of seven report sections, which break the report into distinct areas consisting of one or more lines. Above each section is the section name. (See Figure 4-13.)

Section	Description
Report Header	Contains information to be printed once at the beginning of the report. The report title is displayed in this area.
Page Header	Contains information to be printed at the top of each page. In an ungrouped report, the column headings displaying the field names often are displayed in this area. The Page Header section is empty in the current report.
Group Header	Contains information on groups. This report has two Group Headers: Store ID Header and Department Header. The information in the Group Headers is displayed each time there is a new group.
Detail Section	Contains the records of the table. The field column widths are the same as the column widths set in table design.
Group Footer	There is one Group Footer for each group. The Group Footers often contain formulas that instruct Access to display group totals. In this report, there are totals by Department and by Store ID in the Group Footers.
Page Footer	Contains information to be printed at the bottom of each page, such as the date and page number.
Report Footer	Contains information to be printed once at the end of the report. The current Report Footer includes a grand total for all employees.

You can add fields to a report using **V**iew/Field List. Added field controls are inserted as compound controls. Use Cut and Paste to separate the controls to move them into separate report sections.

The first change you will make is to reorganize the display order of the fields in the report. Notice that the Department Header section displays the label control for each field column, while the Detail section contains the text box control. Report controls are selected and manipulated just like Form controls, but unlike Form controls, the text and label controls are not attached. You will select both controls and move them simultaneously.

■ Select the Employee ID controls in the Department Header and Detail sections.

Hold down ⇧Shift while clicking to select multiple controls.

■ Move the selected controls to the left of the Last Name controls.

■ Next, select all eight controls and move them as a group to the right as shown in Figure 4-14.

■ Clear the selection.

When you are done, your screen should be similar to Figure 4-14.

FIGURE 4-14

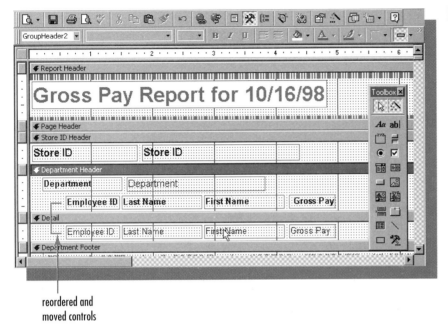

reordered and
moved controls

To see how this change has affected the report, you will preview the report using
Layout Preview.

Concept 4: Layout Preview

There are two ways to view the report as it will appear when printed. You
can use Print Preview to view the entire report page by page. Because this
view displays all the data in the report, it takes longer to generate. This is
the view you have seen whenever a new report is displayed, and is the
view you used when previewing forms.

Another way to view the report is to use Layout Preview to take a
quick look at the report. Layout Preview displays just a sample of the data
in the report so you can quickly check the report's layout. Because it does
not display all the data, it is much quicker to generate.

As a general rule, you should use Print Preview to view the entire report
as it will print. Use Layout Preview for quick checks of design layout. When a
report is large and you just need to check a layout change you have made,
this is the preferred view.

- Select 🔍 Layout Preview from the 🔍▾ View drop-down list.

- If necessary, set the magnification to 75%.

The menu equivalent is **V**iew/La**y**out
Preview.

Your screen should be similar to Figure 4-15.

report in Layout Preview

FIGURE 4-15

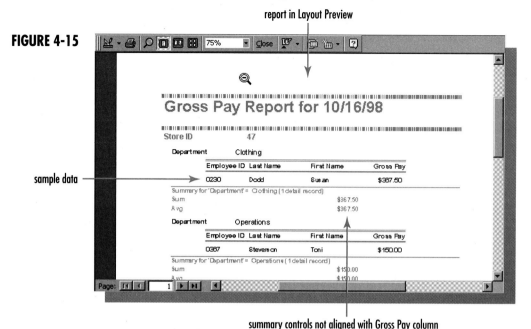

sample data

summary controls not aligned with Gross Pay column

The Layout Preview shows a sample of records in each group as an example of the report layout. The change in the order of the fields improves the organization of the report. However, now you notice that the summary fields for Gross Pay no longer align with the field column. To fix this you will move the controls for the Gross Pay summary fields below the Gross Pay column of data.

- Click ![icon] Design View.

- Scroll the window to see the Department, Store ID, and Report Footer sections.

> **Align the right border of the controls.**

- Select the five Gross Pay summary controls and move them to the right to align with the Gross Pay controls in the Detail section (approximately 5.25" position on the ruler).

Changing Control Properties

The next change you will make is to change how the date is displayed in the Page Footer. Notice that the date control in the Page Footer is =Now(). This is an expression that directs Access to enter the current date maintained on your computer into the report. Each control has property settings that affect how the control looks and acts. By default the property setting associated with the date control displays the date in the Long Date format. To change the date control properties,

> **The menu equivalent is View/Properties, or Properties on the Shortcut menu. You can also double-click a control to display its properties.**

- Select the date control in the Page Footer section.

- Click ![icon] Properties.

Your screen should be similar to Figure 4-16.

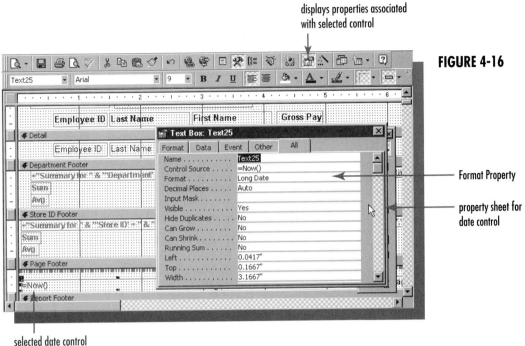

FIGURE 4-16

The property sheet box for the date control is displayed. The All tab displays a list of all properties associated with the selected control. The Format properties contain the same options as in Table Design and vary with the data type of the field. The Format text box displays "Long Date." This date format displays the date as Day, Month xx, 19xx. You want to display the date in the Short Date format of mm/dd/yy.

- ■ Open the Format property drop-down list.

- ■ Select Short Date.

- ■ Close the property sheet.

- ■ Using Layout Preview, preview the changes you have made to the report.

- ■ Scroll to the bottom of page 1.

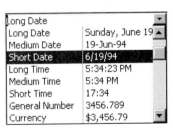

Your screen should be similar to Figure 4-17.

FIGURE 4-17

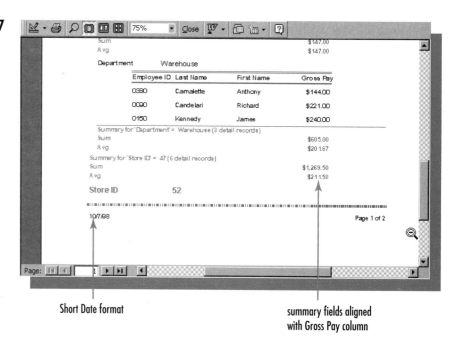

Short Date format   summary fields aligned
                                      with Gross Pay column

The Gross Pay summary fields are aligned with the Gross Pay column of data, and the date appears in the new Short Date format.

■   Return to Design view.

Adding Font, Color, and Line Enhancements

Next, to make the Store ID heading stand out more, you will change the text color and add a heavy colored horizontal line above the controls to help visually separate report areas.

■   Select the Store ID label and text box controls in the Store ID Header section.

■   Select a color of your choice from the [A] Font/Fore Color palette.

■   Click [\] Line.

■   Select [3] 3-pt from the [] Line/Border Width drop-down list.

■   Select the same color as the Store ID controls for the line from the [✎] Line/Border Color palette.

■   Move to the space above the Store ID control and drag from the left margin to the 6.5-inch position on the ruler.

> Do not extend the line beyond the 6.5-inch ruler position or the report width will be too wide to fit on a single page.

Your screen should be similar to Figure 4-18.

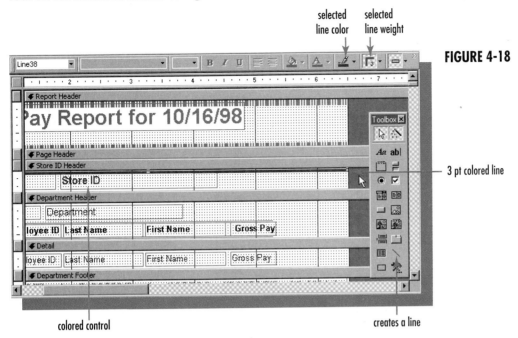

FIGURE 4-18

Finally, you also want to center the title over the report and change the background shading color of the Report Header control.

- Select the report title control (in the Report Header section).

- Drag the title until the left border of the box aligns with the .75-inch ruler mark and the control is centered vertically in the Report Header section (see Figure 4-19).

- Select a color of your choice from the ⬛ ▾ Fill/Back Color palette.

Your screen should be similar to Figure 4-19.

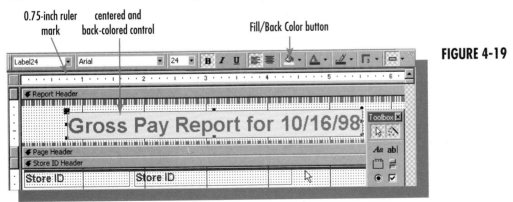

FIGURE 4-19

You are now ready to view your report as it will look when you print it.

- View the report using Print Preview.

- Change the display to view two pages.

Your screen should be similar to Figure 4-20.

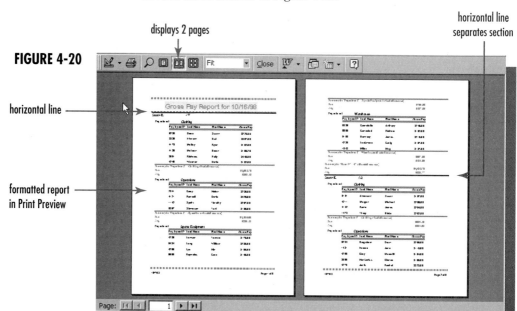

FIGURE 4-20

The title appears centered and with the background color you selected. The color change you made to the Store ID controls and the addition of the colored horizontal line make it much easier to locate the beginning of a new section.

■ Print the entire report.

■ Close the report, saving any layout changes.

■ Close the Gross Pay query.

■ Open the Database window Reports tab.

The names of the two reports you have created are displayed in the Reports object list.

Creating Mailing Labels

Finally, you want to set up a report to print mailing labels for every employee in the Sports Company Employees table. A sample of a mailing label appears below:

Susan Anderson
4389 S. Hayden Rd.
Mesa, AZ 84101

The Report Wizard includes a Label Wizard that will create mailing labels. To use this feature, from the Reports tab,

■ Choose [New] /Label Wizard.

■ Select the Sports Company Employees table from the Table or Query drop-down list.

■ Click [OK].

The Label Wizard dialog box on your screen should be similar to Figure 4-21.

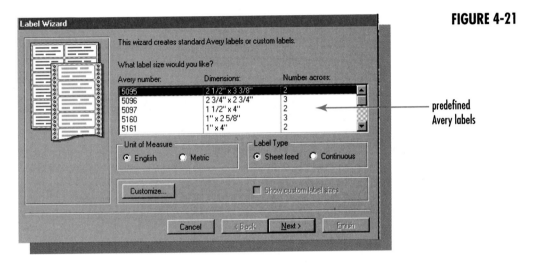

FIGURE 4-21

← predefined Avery labels

In the first Label Wizard dialog box, you specify the type of label you want to create. You can either use a predefined label or create a custom label. The Sports Company uses mailing labels made by Avery, number 5160. These labels appear three across the width of the paper.

■ Select Avery number 5160.

■ Click [Next >].

In this dialog box you specify the font and text color settings for the labels. The default font is Arial and the default font size is 8.

■ If necessary, change the font to Arial and the font size to 10 point.

■ Click [Next >].

> The font settings in this dialog box retain the previous settings chosen using the Label Wizard, so other settings may be displayed.

Just as with other reports, you select the fields from the table to include in the labels. Unlike other reports, however, as you select the fields, you also design the label layout in the Prototype Label box. You may type any additional text, such as punctuation or a holiday message, directly onto the prototype.

■ Add the First Name field to the Prototype Label box.

The dialog box on your screen should be similar to Figure 4-22.

FIGURE 4-22

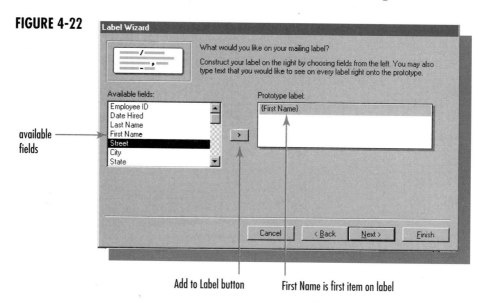

available fields

Add to Label button   First Name is first item on label

The First Name field is displayed in the Prototype Label box. The last name will be on the same line as the first name, separated from the first name by a space. To enter a space to separate the first and last names,

- Press Spacebar.

- Add the Last Name field to the label prototype.

- Press ←Enter.

- To complete the rest of the label, add the Street, City, State, and Zip Code fields to the prototype using the punctuation and spacing shown here.

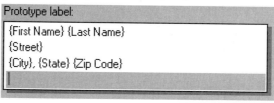

- Click Next >.

In the next dialog box you can specify a field on which to sort the labels. You want to take of advantage of postal discounts resulting from mailings that are sorted by zip code.

- Add the Zip Code field to the Sort By list box.

- Click: Next >.

- Finally enter **Employee Mailing Labels** as the label report name.

- Click [_Finish_].

- Maximize the Print Preview window.

- Zoom the window to 75% to see all three columns of labels.

Your screen should be similar to Figure 4-23.

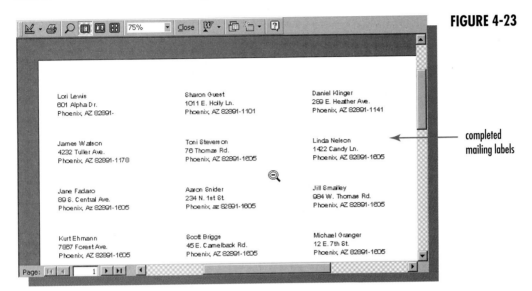

FIGURE 4-23

completed mailing labels

Three columns of mailing labels appear across the width of the page. The placement of the labels on the page corresponds to the 5160 Avery labels you selected using the Label Wizard. The labels are also sorted by zip code, from left to right across the rows, then down the page from top to bottom.

- Print the page of labels that displays your name.

- Close the mailing labels report.

- If you are ready, exit Access.

LAB REVIEW

■ ■ ■ ■ ■ ■ ■ ■ ■ ■

Key Terms

Detail Section (DB156)
group (DB151)
Group Footer (DB156)
Group Header (DB156)
Page Footer (DB156)
Page Header (DB156)
report (DB141)
Report Footer (DB156)
Report Header (DB156)

Command Summary

Command	Toolbar	Action
<u>V</u>iew/La<u>y</u>out Preview	🔍	Displays report layout as it will appear when printed
<u>V</u>iew/<u>P</u>roperties	📝	Displays properties for selected control
<u>V</u>iew/Field <u>L</u>ist		Adds fields to a report
<u>V</u>iew/<u>Z</u>oom	🔍	Changes magnification of Preview window
<u>V</u>iew/P<u>a</u>ges		Changes number of previewed pages
<u>I</u>nsert/<u>R</u>eport		Creates new report

Matching

1. [Summary Options ...] _____   **a.** creates a simple report using all fields in table

2. grouping _____   **b.** displays a sample of how report will appear when printed

3. Page Footer section _____   **c.** allows predefined calculations to be performed in grouped reports

4. Layout Preview _____   **d.** displays entire page in Preview window

5. Report Footer section _____   **e.** contains information that prints at top of first page of report

6. Detail section _____   **f.** part of report that contains table data

7. AutoReport Wizard _____   **g.** contains information that is printed at end of report

8. label prototype _____   **h.** contains information that prints at bottom of each report page

9. Report Header section _____   **i.** used to design the label layout

10. View/Zoom/Fit to Window _____   **j.** arranges data by major categories for clarity and ease of understanding

Fill-In Questions

1. Printed output generated from tables or queries is called a(n) _____.

2. The _____ creates a report that displays all the fields and records from the underlying table or query.

3. The _____ allows you to choose the fields to include in the report.

4. The _____ window displays the report on the screen as it will appear when it is printed.

5. You can display the whole page in the window by adjusting the magnification to _____.

6. Records _____ by categories to allow better analysis of data.

7. Reports that are grouped can contain _____ fields.

8. The calculation that computes the average value for a group is _____.

9. The _____ section of Report Design view contains information to be printed at the top of each page.

10. _____ and _____ can be added to the design of a report to enhance the report's appearance.

Discussion Questions

1. Discuss the advantages of creating reports.

2. Discuss how grouping records in a report makes the report more meaningful.

3. Discuss how queries can be used to create reports. What are the advantages of creating a report from a query?

4. Discuss how group calculations can be used in a report. Give examples of the kinds of information that could benefit from summary data.

Hands-On Practice Exercises

■ ■ ■ ■ ■ ■ ■ ■ ■ ■ ■

Step by Step

Rating System	
☆	Easy
☆☆	Moderate
☆☆☆	Difficult

1. This problem is a continuation of Practice Exercise 4 in Lab 3. James O'Dell at Valley of the Sun Office Supplies is still worried about his inventory and his suppliers. He wants to print a report of all overstocked items so he can encourage his sales staff to push those items.

a. To review James' query that locates the overstocked items, and to help him create a report based on the query, open the Valley of the Sun Office Supplies database you updated in Lab 3, then open the Queries tab and run the Overstocked Items query. Examine the data in the datasheet, then close the Query window.

b. To create James' new report, open the Reports tab, then create a tabular AutoReport based on the Overstocked Items query.

c. Print the report, then close the Report window and save the report as Overstocked Items.

2. This problem is a continuation of Practice Exercise 3 in Lab 3. Michelle at Food for Thought Catering wants to know the sum of all the purchases made by each of her customers. She needs you to help her create a query to find the information and then a report to print it out.

a. Open the Updated Catering Records database you updated in Lab 3. Create a new query and add the Billing and Customers tables to the design grid. Add the Company and the Amount fields to the grid, then save the query as Billing History. Run the query and review the data.

Michelle likes the data, but it does not explain exactly what she wanted to know. The query shows each invoice amount for every customer, but does not give a total of all invoices for every customer. You assure Michelle that you can best retrieve that information by creating a report that groups invoices by company then gives a sum for each company.

b. Close the query datasheet. Create a new report using the Report Wizard. Base the query on the Billing History query you just created, then add all fields in the query to the report.

c. Group the data by company and add a summary option to calculate the sum of the Amount field for each company. You think Michelle could also benefit from knowing what percentage of her business goes to each client, so check the Calculate Percent of Total for Sums box.

d. Select a layout, use portrait orientation, and choose an appropriate style. Name the report Income by Company, then preview the report.

e. As you look through the report, you notice that some company names do not display completely in the text box controls. Modify the report design by adjusting the text box controls and making changes to improve the report appearance, such as lines, text color, boxes, and font changes.

f. Preview, then print the report.

g. Close the Report window, saving any layout changes.

3. This is a continuation of Practice Exercise 5 in Lab 3. Michael at Go West Dude Ranch wants to know how he is spending his money. It seems to disappear quickly every time he does payroll. He also needs to know the total gross payroll per week so he can better budget his money. You assure Michael that you can get all the information he needs by creating a query and a report.

a. Open the Dude Ranch Payroll database you updated in Lab 3, then open the Weekly Paychecks query in Design view. You determine that this query will work well for the report you need, but you need to remove the criteria from the Pay Date column. Remove the criteria, save the query using the same name, and close the Query window.

b. Create a new report using the Report Wizard and base it on the Weekly Paychecks query you just updated. Add the Pay Date, Employee #, First Name, Last Name, and Gross Pay fields to the Selected Fields list box.

c. Group the report by Pay Date (Access will then group the Pay Date by month), then sort it by Pay Date (to divide the weeks within the months).

d. You decide that in addition to knowing the sum of his payroll, Michael might be better able to see how his money is being spent if he knows the average pay of his employees. Add Summary Options to calculate a sum and an average of the pay.

e. Select an appropriate layout, use landscape orientation so all the data will fit, and select a style. Name the report Payroll Summary, then preview the report.

f. Make any changes to adjust the size of controls, and improve the appearance of the report by adding such features as lines, color, and font changes. Then preview the report again. Print the report.

On Your Own

4. This problem is a continuation of Practice Exercise 1 in Lab 3. Debbie at Desert Rescue Cleaning Service wants to do some target marketing, sending flyers to all customers who have at least 10,000 square feet of space. She also wants to know what her average client in Arizona is like. She wants to determine this by examining the average rate and the average square feet of all her Arizona customers. Debbie calls you to help her out.

Open the Desert Rescue Cleaning Service database you updated in Lab 3, then create a new query, named Big Clients, that will select clients with at least 10,000 square feet of space.

After creating the query, you tell Debbie she can use it for many different reports. All she needs right now is mailing labels for those select few big clients. Create mailing labels for Debbie, then print the labels and save the report as Big Clients Labels.

To help Debbie with her other request, you need to create a new report based on the Clients table that will tell Debbie what the average rate and square footage are for all of her Arizona clients. (Hint: You should group the report by state, and format the Square Footage field to standard or fixed.) Make the report look attractive so Debbie can take the report to her next staff meeting. Name the report Average Arizona Clients, then print the report.

⭐⭐☆

5. This problem is a continuation of Practice Exercise 2 in Lab 3. Eddie at TechnoBabble needs his database updated again. Eddie needs a new table that lists his suppliers by code, name, and phone number, and he wants a form to use for data entry.

Using the TechnoBabble Electronics database you updated in Lab 3, create a table of suppliers to hold the information below and make the Supplier field the primary key field. Then create a form, Suppliers, to enter the information.

Supplier	Supplier Name	Phone Number
AMS	American Memory Service	(602) 555-7896
BOC	Balanced Output Company	(303) 555-3426
BTO	Better Tech Offerings	(970) 555-8620
CCR	Crystal Clear Radios	(619) 555-1762
CTC	Cellular Telephone Co.	(202) 555-4139
HSC	Home Security Corp.	(602) 555-8760
LLM	Laser Light Management	(602) 555-5700
MEE	Musical Electronic Engineering	(303) 555-1999

Now that the new information is in the database, Eddie wants to see a report showing the total value of both regular stock items and special order items that are currently on hand, grouped by supplier name and by status. Create a query, named Inventory Status, then a new report, named On Hand Inventory Status Report, to help Eddie find the data he needs. Print the report.

⭐⭐☆

6. This problem is a continuation of Practice Exercise 6 in Lab 3. Open the My Contacts database file you have been working on and last updated in Lab 3.

Create mailing labels for all the contacts in your table. Print the mailing labels.

Create a query and a report of your choice using the data in your database. Print the report.

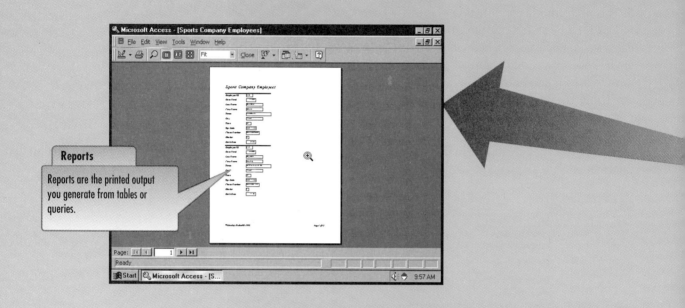

Reports

Reports are the printed output you generate from tables or queries.

Group Calculations

If you group data in your report, you can perform calculations on values, such as a group total, an average, a minimum value, and a maximum value.

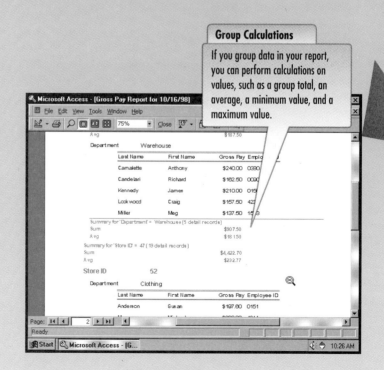

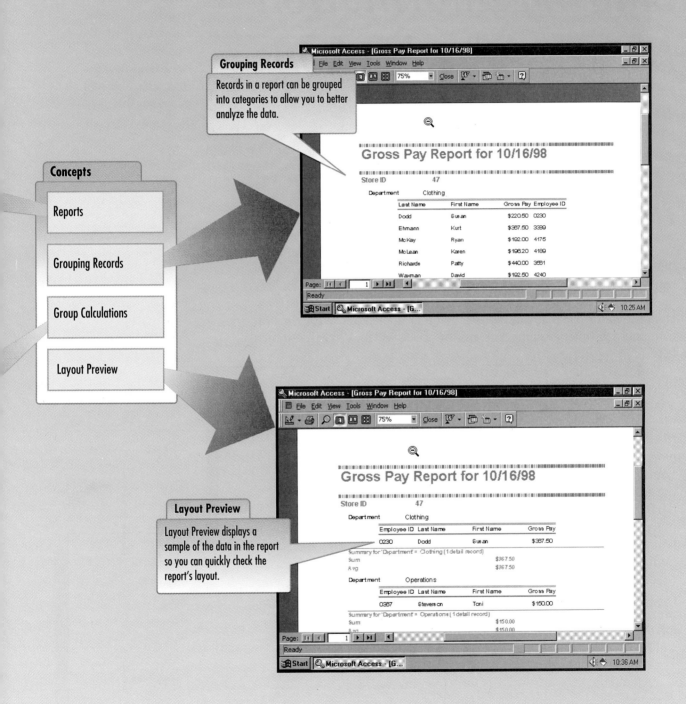

Concepts

- Reports
- Grouping Records
- Group Calculations
- Layout Preview

Grouping Records

Records in a report can be grouped into categories to allow you to better analyze the data.

Layout Preview

Layout Preview displays a sample of the data in the report so you can quickly check the report's layout.

Sharing Information Between Applications

CASE STUDY

You have used Access to obtain information from the Employee database that was requested by the manager. Now you want to include the query results with a brief memo to the manager. To do this you will learn how files created using Access that have their own unique format can be translated into a format that can be used by other applications. Your memo containing the query results generated by Access will look like that shown here.

You have also been asked to create a letter to all employees, offering them a special employee credit card. You have created the letter and will perform a mail merge with data from the Sports Company Employees database to supply the inside address information for the letter. Your completed letter will be similar to that shown here.

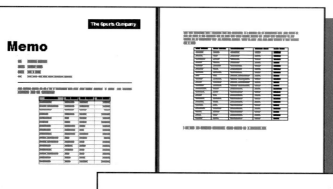

Concept Overview

The following concepts will be introduced in this lab:

1. Copy Between Applications	Information can be copied between applications and if possible is inserted in a format the document can edit.
2. Linked Object	Information that is copied from one file to another as a linked object maintains a connection between the files, allowing the linked object to automatically update when the source file changes.
3. Exporting and Importing	Exporting saves data created using Access in another format, and importing retrieves data that has been saved in another format into an Access table.

Note: This lab assumes that you have completed Lab 3 of Access. You need the database file Sports Company Personnel Records that you saved at the end of Lab 3.

Part 1

Copying Between Applications

The first project you will work on is to create a memo to the manager that contains the list of employees who were hired before 1/1/92.

- ■ Start Access 97.
- ■ Open the Sports Company Personnel Records database from your data disk.
- ■ Open the Pre 1992 Hire Date query.

Note: If an Enter Parameter Value dialog box is displayed, click OK twice to reset the sort order of the Department and Last Name fields in the query datasheet.

- ■ If necessary, maximize the window.

Your screen should be similar to Figure 5-1.

FIGURE 5-1

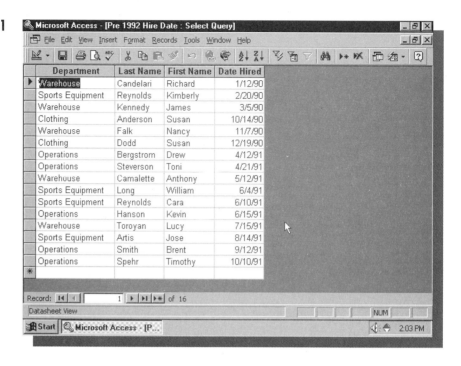

The 16 employees who were hired before January 1, 1992, are listed in the query datasheet. You want to copy the output from the query into a memo to the manager.

Access uses exporting and importing of data to assist in the data transfer between applications.

Concept 1: Copy Between Applications

As with all Office applications, you can cut, copy, and paste selections within and between tables and objects in an Access database. You can also perform these operations between Access databases and other applications. For example, you can copy a database object or selection into a word processing document. The information is inserted in a format the application can edit, if possible.

To do this, you can use Copy and Paste or drag and drop between applications to copy the database object. To use drag and drop, both applications must be open and visible in the window. The memo to the manager has already been created using Word.

■   Load Word and open the document Query Results from your data disk.

Your screen should be similar to Figure 5-2.

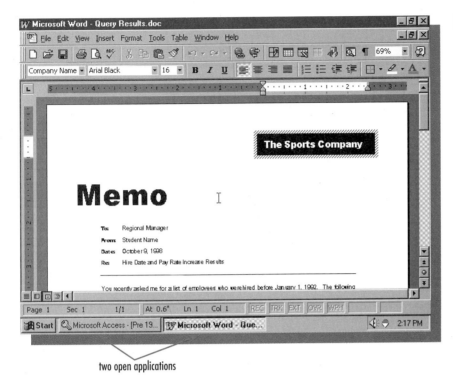

FIGURE 5-2

two open applications

This document contains the text of the memo to the manager.

■ Replace "Student Name" in the memo header with your name.

■ Scroll the memo to read the memo text.

The memo consists of three paragraphs. It also includes blank space between paragraphs where you will enter the information from Access related to the topic discussed in the paragraph.

■ To display both applications at the same time on the desktop, tile the two open applications vertically in the window.

■ Switch to the Access application window and use Edit/Select All Records to select the query datasheet table.

■ Drag the selected table to the space below the first paragraph of the memo in the document.

Right-click the taskbar and choose Tile **V**ertically.

The mouse pointer must be a ⬚ when you drag the selection to copy it.

You could also drag the query object in the Queries tab of the Database window to copy it into the document.

text**DATABASE**

Your screen should be similar to Figure 5-3.

two tiled application windows

FIGURE 5-3

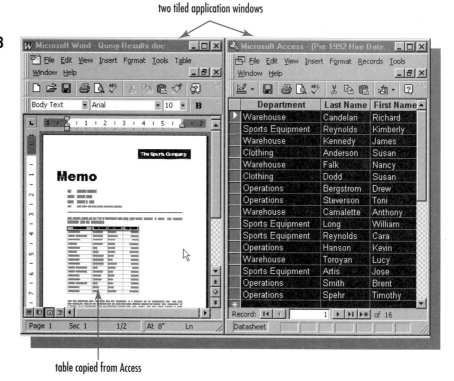

table copied from Access

The query results are copied into the memo document. It is inserted as a format-ted table, having retained the format settings that it had in Access. The table can now be manipulated like any other Word table.

- Undo the vertical window tile.

- Switch to Word and scroll the memo to view the table.

- Select the entire table and center it on the page.

- Create a page break below the table.

To select the table, drag or use **T**able/Select T**a**ble, then click 🔳 to center it.

Right-click the taskbar and select **U**ndo Tile.

Press Ctrl + ↵Enter to create a manual page break.

Linking an Access Object to Another Application

Next you need to insert the query results that calculate the new pay rate for all employees who earn less than $5.50 an hour below the second paragraph of the memo. As you consider the memo, you are concerned that the manager may ask you to modify the query to provide a different analysis of the pay rate increase. If this request is made, you want the memo to be automatically updated when you modify the query. To do this you will link the query object to the memo.

Concept 2: Linked Object

Information created in one application can also be copied into another application as a **linked object**. When an object is linked, the data is stored in the **source file** (the document it was created in). A graphic representation of the data is displayed in the **destination file** (the document in which the object is inserted). A connection between the information in the source file is established by the creation of a link. The link contains references to the location of the source document and to the object within the source document that is linked to the destination document.

When changes are made in the source file that affect the linked object, the changes are automatically reflected in the destination file when it is opened. This is called a **live link**.

When you create linked objects, the date and time on your machine should be accurate. This is because the program refers to the date of the source file to determine whether updates are needed when you open the destination file.

To create a link to the query, you use the ⊞ Insert Database button on the Database toolbar.

■ Display the Database toolbar.

The Database toolbar buttons are identified below.

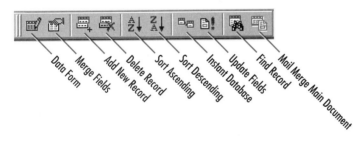

■ Move to below the second paragraph of the memo (located on the second page).

■ Click ⊞ Insert Database.

The Database dialog box on your screen should be similar to Figure 5-4.

FIGURE 5-4

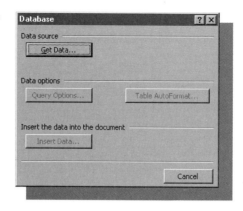

First you need to specify the database file to be inserted into the memo.

- Click  Get Data... .

- If necessary, select the drive containing your data disk from the Look In drop-down list.

- To display Microsoft Access file types, select MS Access Databases from the Files of Type drop-down list.

- Open the file Sports Company Personnel Records.

In the Microsoft Access dialog box, you select the table or query you want to insert in the Word document.

- Open the Queries tab and select Pay Rate Increase.

Notice that the Link to Query option is preselected. This option establishes the link between the query object and the Word document.

- Click   OK   .

creates link to query object

The Database dialog box is displayed again. The Query Options button allows you to modify the query settings. Since you want it to appear as it is, you do not need to use this option. The AutoFormat button lets you select a format to apply to the table. If you do not select a format style, the datasheet is copied into the document as an unformatted table.

> You could also apply a format to the table after it is inserted into the document.

- Click   Table AutoFormat...   .

The Table Autoformat dialog box on your screen should be similar to Figure 5-5.

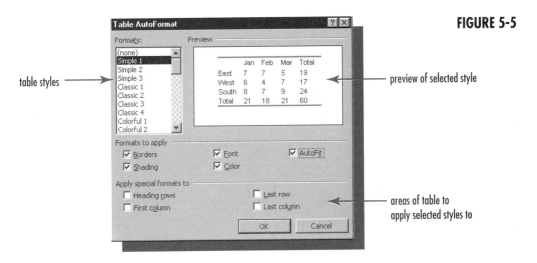

table styles → / preview of selected style → / areas of table to apply selected styles to →

FIGURE 5-5

From this dialog box you select the style you want to use and the parts of the table you want to apply it to.

- ■ Select Heading rows and Last column as the two areas to apply special formats.

- ■ Select a style of your choice.

- ■ Click [OK].

The Database dialog box is displayed again. Finally, to insert the data into the document,

- ■ Click [Insert Data...].

> This text uses the Simple 2 AutoFormat style.

From the Insert Data dialog box, you specify what records to include in the inserted table and whether to insert the data as a field. Inserting it as a field allows the data to be updated whenever the source changes.

- ■ If necessary, select **A**ll.

- ■ Select **I**nsert Data as Field.

- ■ Click [OK].

- ■ Select the table and center it on the page.

- ■ Clear the selection and if necessary scroll the document window to see the entire table.

- ■ If necessary, insert a blank line between the paragraph and the table.

Your screen should be similar to Figure 5-6.

Insert Database button

FIGURE 5-6

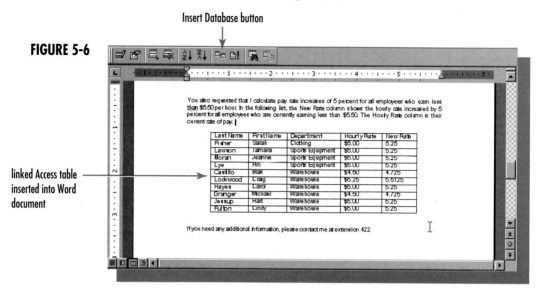

linked Access table
inserted into Word
document

You also requested that I calculate pay rate increases of 5 percent for all employees who earn less than $5.50 per hour. In the following list, the New Rate column shows the hourly rate increased by 5 percent for all employees who are currently earning less than $5.50. The Hourly Rate column is their current rate of pay.

Last Name	First Name	Department	Hourly Rate	New Rate
Fisher	Sarah	Clothing	$5.00	5.25
Lawson	Tamara	Sports Equipment	$5.00	5.25
Moran	Jeanne	Sports Equipment	$5.00	5.25
Lye	Hin	Sports Equipment	$5.00	5.25
Castillo	Blas	Warehouse	$4.50	4.725
Lockwood	Craig	Warehouse	$5.25	5.5125
Hayes	Carol	Warehouse	$5.00	5.25
Granger	Michael	Warehouse	$4.50	4.725
Jessup	Hart	Warehouse	$5.00	5.25
Fulton	Cindy	Warehouse	$5.00	5.25

If you need any additional information, please contact me at extension 422.

The currency format set in query design for the calculated field is not copied to the Word document.

The link to the database file and to the query object is established, and the database table is inserted into the document in the selected format style. The table lists the 10 employees who earn less than $5.50 and their new rates of pay.

You dropped off a copy of the memo to the manager, and after a short time, you receive a call asking you to include employees who are earning $5.50 and to increase the pay rate percentage from 5 percent to 7.5 percent. To make these changes, you need to modify the query design.

- Switch to Access.

- Open the Pay Rate Increase query in Design view.

- Change the Hourly Rate criterion to <=5.50.

- Change the New Rate formula to calculate the increase at 7.5 percent.

- Run the query.

The query datasheet now lists 21 employees who earn $5.50 or less, and also lists their new pay rate based on a 7.5 percent increase.

- Save the query using the same name.

If you were opening the Word document, the changes would be automatically updated.

- Switch to Word.

The Word table has not changed to reflect the changes made in the source file.
To update data in the fields,

■ Click anywhere in the table to select it.

■ Click 🖹 Update Fields (in the Database toolbar).

■ Select the entire table and center it on the page.

■ Clear the selection.

> You can also press F9 or choose Update Field on the Shortcut menu. The object must be selected when you update it.

Your screen should be similar to Figure 5-7.

Update Fields button

FIGURE 5-7

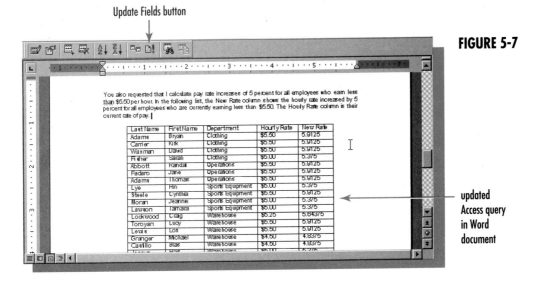

updated Access query in Word document

The table is redrawn to include the new records and now reflects the data in the revised query.

■ Update the memo text in the paragraph above the table to reflect the change in data shown in the table.

■ Save the memo using the file name Revised Query Results.

■ Print the document.

■ Close the Database toolbar.

■ Exit Word.

■ Close the Pay Rate Increase query.

The Database window should be displayed.

Exporting Access Data to Excel

Next you want to copy the Gross Pay for 10/16/98 query datasheet to an Excel workbook so that you can perform additional mathematical analysis on the data. Rather than opening the query, you can simply select the query object name from the Queries tab and save it to an external file in an Excel file format.

Concept 3: Exporting and Importing

Exporting saves data created using Access in another format to be inserted into a document created in a different application. **Importing** retrieves data that has been saved in another format into an Access table. There are many different types of file formats. Access will import and export data in the following formats.

- Text files (.asc, .txt, .csv, .tab)—These include delimited text and fixed-width text.

Delimited text is a file containing values separated by commas, tabs, semicolons, or other characters, as in the following example: 1/12/89 0:00:00,"Candelari","Richard".
Fixed-width text is a file containing values arranged so that each field has a certain width, as in the following example: 1/12/89 0:00:00 Candelari Richard.

- Rich text format (.rtf)—a file format that retains all the format settings such as font, alignment, and number formatting for column heads and data as shown below.

Date Hired	Last Name	First Name
1/12/89	Candelari	Richard
2/20/89	Reynolds	Kimberly
3/5/89	Kennedy	James

- Excel versions 3.0, 4.0, 5.0, 7.0/95 and 8.0/97 (.xls)
- Lotus 1-2-3 .wk1, and .wk3 formats
- Paradox releases 3.x, 4.x and 5.0 (.pdx)
- FoxPro versions 2.x and 3.0 (.dbf)
- dBase III, III+, IV, and 5 (.dbf)
- HTML versions 1.1, 2.0, 3.x

Access can import files saved in any of these formats and converts the information into an Access table. Access files that are exported to any of these formats can be read and used by any programs that use these formats.

The Save As/Export command on the File menu is used to convert database objects into the different file formats that can be used in other applications.

- ■ Select (highlight) the Gross Pay for 10/16/98 query object.

- ■ Choose File/Save As/Export/ OK .

The dialog box on your screen should be similar to Figure 5-8.

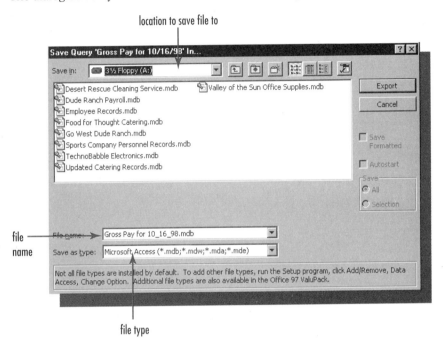

location to save file to

file name

file type

FIGURE 5-8

From the Save Query In dialog box, you specify the name and location to save the new file and the type of file you want it saved as. In addition, you can specify whether you want to include the original file formatting in the new file and if you want to have the exported file automatically opened in the selected application. You will save the query as an Excel 97 file format to your data disk preserving the original table formats such as fonts and field widths. You will also have the new application load automatically and display the new file.

- ■ If necessary, select the drive containing your data disk as the location to save the file.

- ■ Open the Save as Type drop-down list box and select Microsoft Excel 97.

- ■ Select Save Formatted.

- ■ Select Autostart.

- ■ Click Export.

The database query is saved to a file in an Excel file format and Excel is loaded.

Your screen should be similar to Figure 5-9.

FIGURE 5-9

field names

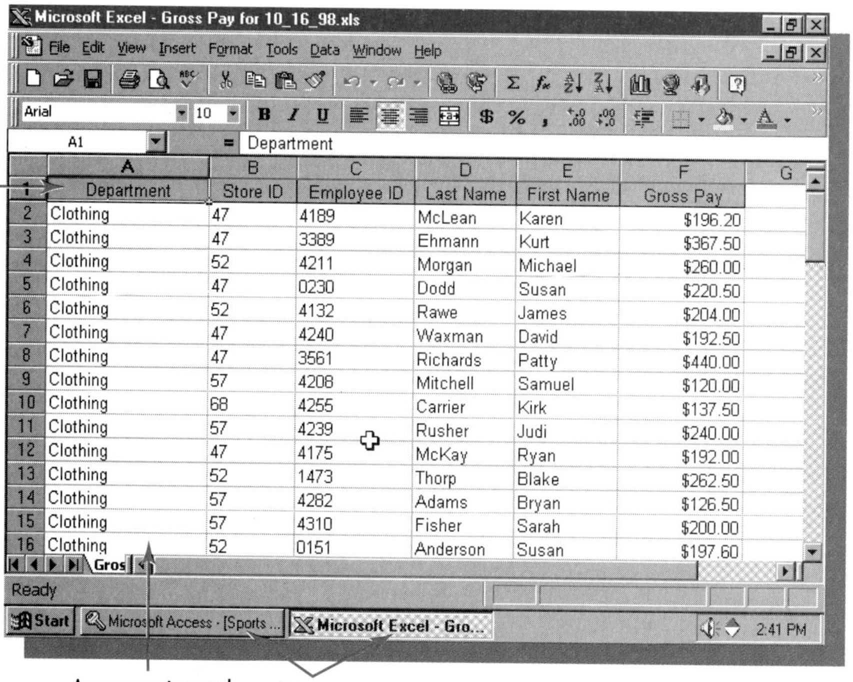

Access query imported into Excel

two open applications

The new workbook file is open with the information from the query displayed in it. The field names are placed in the first row of the spreadsheet, and the data begins in row 2. The column heads and column widths are formatted as they appeared in the query datasheet. Now the data can be manipulated using Excel commands and features. For example, it would be easy to calculate total and average values by departments.

Click ∑ to sum the Gross Pay column.

■ Display a grand total of the Gross Pay column in cell F75.

The changes you have made to the worksheet do not affect the Access table from which the data was obtained.

■ Print the worksheet.

■ Save the worksheet using the same file name.

■ Exit Excel.

Part 2

Creating a Mail Merge Using Word and Access

Note: It is helpful if you have completed the Merge section of Lab 4 of Word 97. If you have not, read the information in that section to become familiar with the procedure before completing the following section.

The Sports Company has also decided to send all its employees a Sports Company credit card. The body of the letter to accompany the credit cards has already been created and saved as Employee Credit Card Letter on your data disk. You want the letter to display each employee's name and address information as an inside address and to include the first name in the salutation.

This data is maintained in the Sports Company Employees table. To include this information for each employee in the letter, you will perform a mail merge between Word and Access.

First you will need to create a query to include all fields needed in the inside address.

- Using the Sports Company Employees table, create a query named Employee Address that will display each employee's first name, last name, street, city, state, and zip code (in that order).

To help in sorting the mail, you want the merged letters to appear in sorted order by zip code. Because you also want to test the merge with a small amount of records, you will also limit the scope of the query to employees in the city of Chandler.

- Set the sort order of the Zip Code field to ascending.

- Enter Chandler in the City criteria field.

- Then, to include your record in the query output, in the OR row of the grid enter your first and last name in the appropriate criteria fields.

Your screen should be similar to Figure 5-10.

FIGURE 5-10

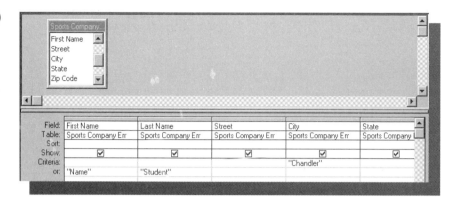

- Run the Query.

- If the query output does not display three records with a city of Chandler and your record, fix the query grid criteria to achieve the correct results.

- Save the query as Employee Address.

- Close the Query window.

The Mail Merge feature is used to insert field data from an Access table into a Word document. Performing a mail merge between Access and Word is part of the automated Office Links feature. The 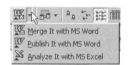 Office Links drop-down list button includes three choices:

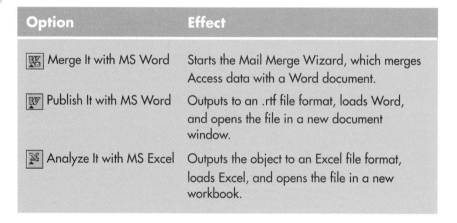

> Merge It is the default Office Links button.

Option	Effect
Merge It with MS Word	Starts the Mail Merge Wizard, which merges Access data with a Word document.
Publish It with MS Word	Outputs to an .rtf file format, loads Word, and opens the file in a new document window.
Analyze It with MS Excel	Outputs the object to an Excel file format, loads Excel, and opens the file in a new workbook.

To merge the address data in the query with a Word document,

> The menu equivalent is **T**ools/Office **L**inks/**M**erge It.

- Select the Employee Address query object, if necessary.

> You can also begin a mail merge from within Word.

- Click **M**erge It with MS Word/ OK .

The Microsoft Word Mail Merge Wizard dialog box is displayed. Your first step is to indicate whether you will use an existing document (the default) or whether you will need a new doccument. To accept the default,

■ Click [OK].

The Select Microsoft Word Document dialog box appears next.

■ If necessary, select the drive containing your data disk as the location.

■ Select Employee Credit Card Letter.

■ Click [Open].

■ If necessary, maximize the application window.

Your screen should be similar to Figure 5-11.

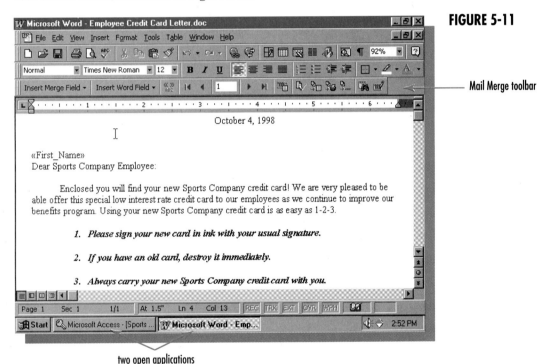

FIGURE 5-11

— Mail Merge toolbar

two open applications

Word is loaded, and the Employee Credit Card Letter document is opened. In addition, the Mail Merge toolbar is displayed. These buttons are identified below.

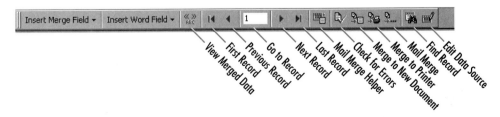

■ If necessary, dock the Mail Merge toolbar below the Formatting toolbar.

DATABASE

Next you need to enter the merge fields in the letter to create the inside address. This is similar to creating a mailing label prototype. The first merge field you will specify will display the employee's first name in the inside address.

- Move to the line above the salutation (Ln 4).
- Click Insert Merge Field ▾ .
- Select First_Name.

Your screen should be similar to Figure 5-12.

FIGURE 5-12

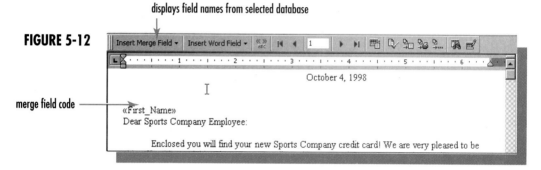

- Continue to select the field names to add the merge fields to the letter using the punctuation and spacing shown in Figure 5-13.
- Insert two blank lines above the salutation.

The last change you need to make to the document is to insert each employee's first name in place of "Sports Company Employee" in the salutation.

- Replace the text "Sports Company Employee" with the First Name merge field.

Your screen should be similar to Figure 5-13.

FIGURE 5-13

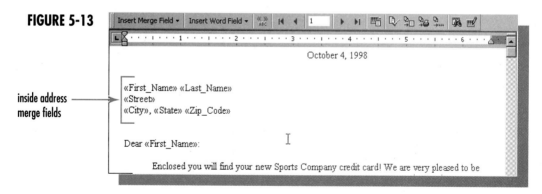

You are now ready to merge the addresses from Access into the Word document.

■   Click 🔲 Merge to New Document.

The menu equivalent is **T**ools/Mail Mer**g**e/**M**erge/**M**erge.

Your screen should be similar to Figure 5-14.

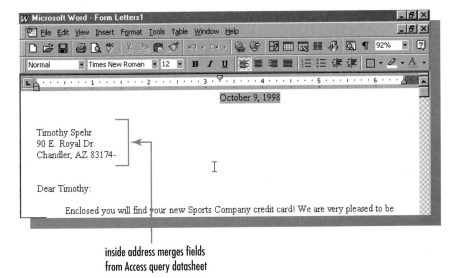

FIGURE 5-14

inside address merges fields
from Access query datasheet

After a few seconds, Word displays the first personalized letter. The field information from the first record in the query replaces the appropriate merge field codes. The merge fields create a link to the Access database and query. Whenever needed, you can reopen the Word document to print a batch of letters using the current data in the Access table.

■   Scroll the file to view the other letters.

■   Print the letter displaying your information only.

■   Close the merge document without saving it.

■   Save the merge form letter document as Employee Credit Card Letter Merge.

■   Exit Word and Access.

LAB REVIEW

■ ■ ■ ■ ■ ■ ■ ■ ■ ■ ■ ■

Key Terms

destination file   (DB177)
export   (DB182)
import   (DB182)
linked object   (DB177)
live link   (DB177)
source file   (DB177)

Command Summary

Command	Button	Action
Tools/Office**L**inks/**M**erge It	🔲	Starts the Word Mail Merge

Fill-In Questions

1. Data that is _____ has been saved in another format into an Access table.

2. _____ saves data created using Access in another format.

3. Text that is _____ contains values separated by commas.

4. When an object is _____, the data is stored in the source document.

5. When a document has a(n) _____, changes are automatically reflected in the destination document.

Discussion Questions

1. Discuss the difference between importing and exporting data. Give examples of how each could be used.

2. Discuss the types of formats in which Access can save data. What feature is used to save data in a different format?

3. Discuss the differences between fixed-width and delimited text. Give examples of how data would be displayed with each type.

4. Discuss how an object can be linked from Access to another application. Discuss how a live link works.

Hands-On Practice Exercises

■ ■ ■ ■ ■ ■ ■ ■ ■ ■ ■ ■

Step by Step	**Rating System**	☆	Easy
		☆☆	Moderate
		☆☆☆	Difficult

☆

1. This problem is a continuation of Practice Exercise 4 in Lab 3. James O'Dell, the manager of the Valley of the Sun Office Supplies company, has asked you for an inventory report on all supplies whose cost is over $3.00 and quantity is more than 50.

  a. Open the Valley of the Sun Office Supplies database and create a query that displays the item number, item name, and price of all products that have a quantity on hand greater than 50 and are priced over $3.00.

  b. Save the query as Stock with Quantities over 50.

  c. Open Word and enter the following text.

> TO: James Green
> FROM: [your name]
> DATE: [current date]
>
> Below is the information you requested on inventory.

  d. Copy the query results into the Word document.

  e. Save the memo as Stock On Hand. Print the document.

☆☆

2. To complete this problem, you will use the Sports Company Personnel Records database. The Sports Company wants to invite all employees who have worked for the company since before 1992 to a special recognition luncheon. You have been asked to write invitations to these employees.

  a. Open the Sports Company Personnel Records database file and select the Pre 1992 Hire Date query object.

  b. Load Word and create the following memo.

> To: **Sports Company Employee**
> From: [your name]
> Date: [current date]

You are cordially invited to a luncheon in honor of all employees who have worked for The Sports Company since before 1992. The luncheon will be held at the Corporate Center on May 25. Please RSVP to your department manager by May 20.

  c. Save the memo as Employee Luncheon.

  d. Merge the first and last names of the employees from the query in place of the "Sports Company Employee" text in the memo.

  e. Print one of the merged letters. Do not save the merged document. Resave the memo.

☆☆

3. This problem is a continuation of Practice Exercise 5 in Lab 3. The Dude Ranch Payroll Service Company has recently introduced several new services. You have been asked to write a letter to all Phoenix customers announcing the new services.

  a. Open the database and create a query that contains the name and address information of all customers whose city is Phoenix.

b. Open Word and create the following letter:

[current date]

Dear Customer:

The Dude Ranch Payroll Company is offering several new services described in the enclosed brochure. In appreciation for your business and as an incentive to try one of our new services, enclosed you will find a voucher for a 5 percent discount on the cost of our new services.

We hope to hear from you soon.

Sincerely,

[your name]

c. Save the letter as Dude Ranch New Services.

d. Enter merge fields in appropriate locations in the Word document. Merge the addresses from the Access query into the Word document. Print one letter from the merged document.

e. Do not save the merged document.

On Your Own

4. Debbie of Desert Rescue Cleaning Service would like you to create a letter to be sent to all her customers. Use the Desert Rescue Cleaning Service database for the names and addresses to be included in the letter. The letter should thank the customers for their loyalty and offer them a 10% discount for recommending another customer to Desert Rescue Cleaning Service. Merge the addresses from the database into the letter you create. Save and print the letters.

5. Using the Sports Company Personnel Records database, export the Pay Rate Increase query to Excel. In Excel, calculate the average Hourly Rate and New Rate by department and for all employees. Add a worksheet title. Include your name and the current date in a subtitle. Print the worksheet.

5 Sharing Information Between Applications

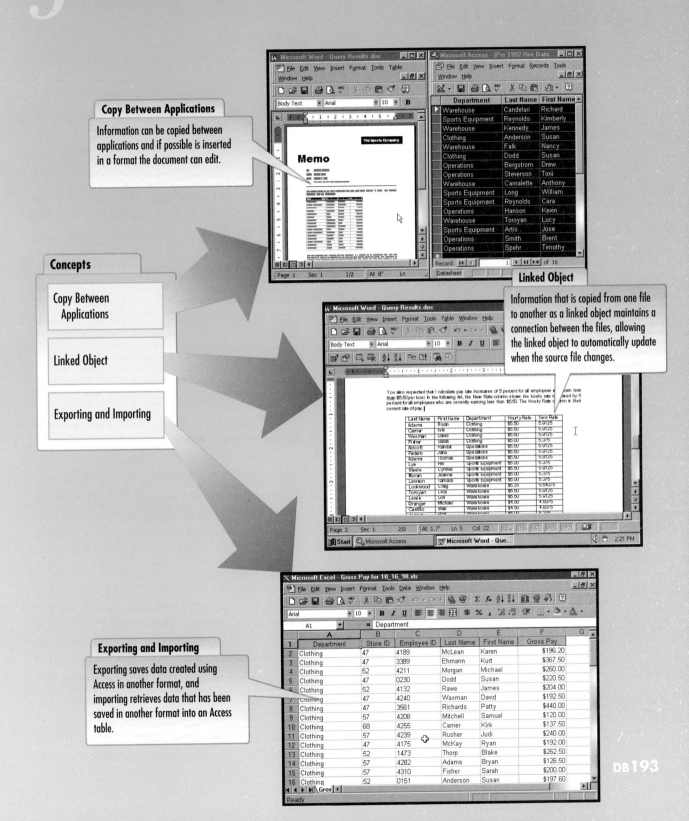

Copy Between Applications

Information can be copied between applications and if possible is inserted in a format the document can edit.

Concepts

Copy Between Applications

Linked Object

Exporting and Importing

Linked Object

Information that is copied from one file to another as a linked object maintains a connection between the files, allowing the linked object to automatically update when the source file changes.

Exporting and Importing

Exporting saves data created using Access in another format, and importing retrieves data that has been saved in another format into an Access table.

Case Project

Introduction

This project is designed to reinforce your knowledge of the database features used in the Access labs. You will also be expected to use the Office Assistant to learn more about advanced features available in Access.

Case

Marianne Virgili is the Director of the Glenwood Springs Chamber Resort Association. She has asked you to create a database file of the Chamber members.

Part I

In this section you will create the tables that will make up your database.

   a. On paper, design a table to hold information about the Chamber members. The table should include a membership number, the business name, address (including street, city, state, and zip code), a telephone number, and contact name.

   b. On paper, design a table to hold the types of businesses that belong to the Chamber Resort Association. This table should include the membership number, type of business, and the number of employees the business employs. (Hint: Companies employ a single number of employees, for example, "1" or "50", not "1 to 50.")

   c. On paper, design a table to hold the dues payments for the Chamber members. This table should include the membership number, the date the payment is due, and the amount of the payment. The amount of payment is based on the number of employees the company employs. The companies are divided into three categories: small (1 to 20 employees), medium (21 to 60 employees), and large (61 or more employees). Small companies' dues are $200, medium are $300, and large are $500.

   d. In Access create a database to hold the three tables.

   e. From your paper designs, create the three tables. Add descriptions to fields that do not have field names that fully describe how the data should be entered. Change the field widths and properties as necessary. Create primary key fields. Save the tables using appropriate names.

f. Create a customized form for each of the tables.

g. Use the customized forms to enter 25 members into the tables. (Add yourself as one of the company names.) Be sure to enter the same membership number for each individual member so the records can be joined in queries and reports. Also remember that the number of employees determines the payment amount due.

Part II

You will use the tables you created in Part I to create queries on the data.

a. Create a query that shows the membership number, member name, and the city. Sort the query by city.

b. Print the query datasheet.

c. Create a query that shows the types of businesses that belong to the Chamber Resort Association, along with the name, membership number, and number of employees they employ.

d. Sort the query by type of business and membership number.

e. Save the query as Member Type.

f. Print the query datasheet.

g. Create a query to display the members that employ more than 50 employees. Display any fields you feel would be appropriate in a report that contains this data.

h. Print the query datasheet.

Part III

In this section you will create reports from the data in your tables.

a. Create a customized report that shows the due date for all members whose dues are due from the current date to two months from now. Include any fields you feel would be appropriate for this report. Use groups if necessary and add an appropriate title.

b. Print the report.

c. Open the saved query Member Type. Create a customized report from the query. Group the report by type of business.

d. Print the report.

e. Create a customized report that groups the companies by categories (small, medium, and large). Total the dues payments for each group and display the percentage for each group. Include the members' names and any other fields that you feel are appropriate.

f. Print the report.

Glossary of Key Terms

Best Fit: A feature that automatically adjusts column width to fit the longest entry.

Bound control: A control that is tied to a field in an underlying table.

Calculated control: A control on a form or report that displays the result of a calculation.

Calculated field: A field that displays the result of a calculation in a query.

Character string: A group of characters.

Cell: The space created by the intersection of a vertical column and a horizontal row.

Column selector bar: In Query Design view, the thin gray bar just above the field name in the grid.

Column width: The number of characters that are displayed in a field column in Datasheet view.

Comparison operator: A symbol used in expressions that allows you to make comparisons. The > (greater than) and < (less than) symbols are examples of comparison operators.

Compound control: Two related controls, such as a text box control and its associated label control.

Control: In Form and Report Design views, a graphical object that can be selected and modified.

Criteria: Specific set of limiting conditions that you want records to meet in order to be displayed in a query, form, or report.

Criteria expression: An expression that will select only the records that meet certain limiting criteria.

Current record: The record, containing the insertion point, that will be affected by the next action.

Data type: Attribute for a field that determines what type of data it can contain.

Database: An organized collection of related information.

Design grid: The lower part of the Query Design window, which displays settings that are used to define the query.

Destination file: The document in which a linked object is inserted.

Detail section: Section of Form and Report Design that contains the records of the table.

Docked: A toolbar or menu bar that appears in a separate window that is fixed to an edge of the Access window.

Edit mode: In Datasheet view, when an insertion point is displayed.

Export: To save data created using Access in another format.

Expression: Description of acceptable values in a validity check, which can contain any combination of the following elements: operators, identifiers, and values.

Field: A single category of data in a table, the values of which appear in a column of a datasheet.

Field list: A small window that lists all fields in an underlying table.

Field name: Label used to identify the data stored in a field.

Field property: An attribute of a field that affects its appearance or behavior.

Field selector: A small gray box or bar in datasheets and queries that can be clicked to select the entire column. The field selector usually contains the field names.

Field size: Field property that limits a text data type to a certain size or limits numeric data to values within a specific range.

Filter: A restriction placed on records in an open form or datasheet to temporarily isolate a subset of records.

Filter by Form: This feature provides a blank version of the current form or datasheet. Values are typed into the blank form or selected from a pull-down list. Records are filtered based on the values entered into the blank form.

Filter by Selection: A type of filter that displays only records containing a specific value.

Floating: A toolbar or menu bar that appears in a separate window that can be moved by dragging.

Font: The typeface, size, and style of printed characters.

Form: A database object used primarily for data entry and making changes to existing records.

Form Footer: Section of Form and Report design that may display information such as instructions, notes, or grand totals.

Form Header: Section of Form and Report design that may display information such as a title, instructions, or graphics.

Group: A way of organizing data on a common attribute. When data is grouped, calculations can be performed on all data in each group.

Group Footer: Section of Report Design that contains information such as group totals to be printed below each group.

Group Header: Section of Report Design that contains information to be printed at the beginning of each group.

Identifier: A part of an expression that refers to the value of a field, control, or property.

Import: To retrieve data that has been saved in another format into an Access table.

Inner join: The default join between tables; based on common fields if one of the common fields is a primary key.

Input mask: Used in fields and text boxes to format data and provide control over what values can be entered into a field.

Join: An association between tables that tells Access how data between tables is related.

Label control: A control found on a form or report that displays descriptive titles, instructions, or notes.

Landscape: Printing orientation that prints a report across the length of the page.

Linked object: An object that is pasted into another application. The data is stored in the source document, and a graphic representation of the data is displayed in the destination document.

Literal character: In an input mask, a character such as the parentheses surrounding the area code of a telephone number, or a hyphen used to separate the parts of a telephone number.

Live link: When the source document is edited, the changes are automatically reflected in the destination document.

Many-to-many relationship: Records in both tables can have many matching records in the other table.

Mask character: In an input mask, a symbol that controls where and what type of data is entered in a field.

Move handle: Used to move menu bars and toolbars to a new location.

Multitable query: A query that uses more than one table.

Navigation buttons: Used to move through records in Datasheet and Form views. Also available in the Print Preview window.

Navigation mode: In Datasheet view, when the entire field is highlighted.

Object: A table, form, or report that can be selected and manipulated as a unit.

Object tab: In the Database window, used to select the type of object.

Office Assistant: Used to get help on features specific to the Office application you are using.

One-to-many relationship: Records in one table can have many matching records in a second table, but the second table can have only one match in the first table.

One-to-one relationship: Records in both tables have only one matching record.

Operator: A symbol or word that indicates that an operation is to be performed.

Orientation: The direction the paper prints, either landscape or portrait.

Page Footer: Section of Report Design that contains information to be printed at the bottom of each page.

Page Header: Section of Report Design that contains information to be printed at the top of each page. The column headings displaying the field names are displayed in this area.

Point: A measurement of the height of characters. One point equals approximately 1/72 inch.

Portrait: Printing orientation that prints the report across the width of a page.

Primary key: One or more fields in a table that uniquely identify a record.

Query: Used to view data in different ways, to analyze data, and to change data.

Query datasheet: Where the result or answer to a query is displayed.

Record: A row of a table, consisting of a group of related fields.

Record number indicator: A small box that displays the current record number in the lower left corner of most views. The record number indicator is surrounded by the navigation buttons.

Record selector: Displayed to the left of the first column; it can be used to select an entire record in Datasheet view.

Referential integrity: Rules that are used to preserve the defined relationships between tables when you enter or delete records in tables that are joined.

Relationship: A link made between tables, usually through at least one common field.

Report: Printed output generated from queries or tables.

Report Footer: Section of Report Design that contains information to be printed once at the end of the report.

Report Header: Section of Report Design that contains information to be printed once at the beginning of the report. By default, the report title and date are displayed in this area.

Sizing handles: Boxes that surround a selected object that can be used to adjust the size of the object.

Sort: A temporary record order in the Datasheet that reorders records in a table.

Source file: The document in which a linked object is created.

Tab order: The order in which Access moves through a form or table when the `Tab ⇆` key is pressed.

Table: Consists of vertical columns and horizontal rows of information about a particular category of things.

Text box control: A control on a form or report that displays data from a table or query.

Typeface: The appearance and shape of characters, such as Times Roman and Courier.

Unbound control: A control that is not tied to a field in an underlying table.

Validation text: Text that is displayed when a validation rule is violated.

Validity check: A check that Access performs to see whether data meets certain criteria.

Value: A part of an expression that is a number, date, or character.

View: An Access window format for viewing objects in a database.

Wildcard character: Placeholder for other characters when using Find and Replace, queries, filters, and expressions.

Workspace: The center area of the window where different Access windows display as you are using the program.

Command
Summary

Command	Shortcut	Toolbar	Action
File/**N**ew Database	Ctrl + N		Creates a new database
File/**O**pen Database	Ctrl + O		Opens existing database
File/**C**lose	Ctrl + W		Closes open window
File/**S**ave	Ctrl + S		Saves table
File/Save **A**s/Export			Saves a database object with a new name
File/Page Set**u**p/Landscape			Changes page orientation to Landscape
File/Print Pre**v**iew			Displays file as it will appear when printed
File/**P**rint	Ctrl + P		Prints contents of file
File/E**x**it	Alt + F4		Closes Access and returns to Windows 95 desktop
Edit/U**n**do	Ctrl + Z		Cancels last action
Edit/Cu**t**	Ctrl + X or Delete		Deletes selected record
Edit/Se**l**ect Record	⇧Shift + Spacebar		Selects current record
Edit/Select **A**ll	Ctrl + A		Selects all controls on a form in Form Design view
Edit/**F**ind	Ctrl + F		Locates specified data
Edit/R**e**place	Ctrl + H		Locates and replaces specified data
Edit/Delete Colu**m**ns	Delete		Removes selected column from design grid
Edit/Delete **R**ows			Deletes selected field from table in Design view
Edit/Primary **K**ey			Defines a field as a primary key field
Edit/Cle**a**r Grid			Clears all fields from design grid

Command	Shortcut	Toolbar	Action
View/**D**esign View			Displays the Design view window
View/**F**orm View			Displays the Form view window
View/Data**s**heet View			Displays the Datasheet view window
View/La**y**out Preview			Displays sample report layout as it will appear when printed
View/Print Pre**v**iew			Displays table, form, query, or report as it will appear when printed
View/**Z**oom			Changes magnification of Preview window
View/P**a**ges			Changes number of previewed pages
View/**P**roperties			Displays properties for selected control
View/Field **L**ist			Adds fields to a report
View/**T**otals		Σ	Displays Total row in Query design grid
Insert/**F**ield			Inserts a new field in table in Design view
Insert/**R**eport			Creates new report
Filte**r**/Appl**y** Filter/Sort			Applies filter to table
Query/**R**un			Displays query results in Query Datasheet view
Query/Show T**a**ble			Displays Show Table dialog box
F**o**rmat/**C**olumn Width			Changes width of table columns in Datasheet view
F**o**rmat/**C**olumn Width/**B**est Fit			Sizes selected columns to accommodate longest entry or column heading
F**o**rmat/**H**ide Columns			Hides columns in Datasheet view
F**o**rmat/**U**nhide Columns			Redisplays hidden columns in Datasheet view
F**o**rmat/A**l**ign/**L**eft			Aligns selected controls to left
F**o**rmat/**S**ize/To **F**it			Automatically resizes a control to fit contents
F**o**rmat/**V**ertical Spacing/Make **E**qual			Equalizes vertical space between selected multiple controls
Records/**F**ilter/**F**ilter by Form			Displays blank datasheet for entering values to be displayed
Records/**F**ilter/Filter by **S**election			Displays only records that contain a specific value

DATABASE

Command	Shortcut	Toolbar	Action
Records/**S**ort/**A**scending		[A↓Z]	Reorders records in ascending alphabetical order
Records/**R**emove Filter/Sort		[▽]	Removes sort order or filter and redisplays original records and order
Records/**D**ata Entry			Hides existing records and displays the Data Entry window
Tools/**R**elationships			Defines a permanent relationship between tables
Tools/OfficeLinks/**M**erge It		[▧]	Starts the Word Mail Merge
Window/**1** <name>			Displays selected window

Index

Notes

DB212 Notes